FULL
of
HEART

Center Point
Large Print

**This Large Print Book carries the
Seal of Approval of N.A.V.H.**

FULL
of
HEART

My Story of Survival, Strength, and Spirit

J. R. MARTINEZ
with
Alexandra Rockey Fleming

CENTER POINT LARGE PRINT
THORNDIKE, MAINE

This Center Point Large Print edition is published in the year 2013 by arrangement with Hyperion.

The text of this Large Print edition is unabridged.
In other aspects, this book may
vary from the original edition.
Printed in the United States of America
on permanent paper.
Set in 16-point Times New Roman type.

ISBN: 978-1-61173-617-5

Library of Congress Cataloging-in-Publication Data

Martinez, J. R. (Jose Rene), 1983–
Full of heart : my story of survival, strength, and spirit / J. R. Martinez
    with Alexandra Rockey Fleming.
    p. cm.
ISBN 978-1-61173-617-5 (library binding : alk. paper)
1. Martinez, J. R. (Jose Rene), 1983–
    2. Disabled veterans—United States—Biography.
    3. Iraq War, 2003–2011—Veterans—Biography.
    4. All my children (Television program)
    5. Dancing with the stars (Television program)
    6. United States. Army—Biography.
    7. Salvadoran Americans—Biography.
    I. Fleming, Alexandra Rockey. II. Title.
UB363.M36 2012b
362.4092—dc23
[B]
                                                        2012035182

For my sister Consuelo,
whom I love very much,

and for my beautiful daughter,
Lauryn Anabelle,

and in memory of my sister Anabel,
who left far too early but remains in our hearts

FULL
of
HEART

CONTENTS

May 2003

"Whenever you're ready."

My nurse, Mike, pointed to the mirror in front of me.

It had been twenty-six days since I'd hit the roadside bomb on a road in Iraq, twenty-six days since I'd been medevacked to Landstuhl, Germany, the largest military medical center outside the United States, and then here, to the burn unit at Brooke Army Medical Center at Fort Sam Houston in San Antonio, Texas.

"You won't see the same face you remember from before," said Mike. "But it's going to get better. Just know that."

People had admired my looks all my life. My bright smile. My soft, curly hair. I didn't ask for the compliments, but I came to expect them. I got used to being the guy everyone looked at. Now, after suffering third-degree burns over 34 percent of my body, including my face, hands, and torso, I needed to look at myself.

My eyes met the mirror. My heart jumped. I

blinked and turned away. *That's you,* I thought. *You have to look.* I forced myself to turn back.

As a kid I'd been terrified by the disfigured slasher Freddy Krueger in the *Nightmare on Elm Street* film series. Now he was here, in this hospital room, looking out at me from my own reflection.

I pushed the mirror away.

Mike reached out to put his hand on my shoulder. "I know this isn't what you expected to see, but you're not going to look like this for the rest of your life."

Rage bubbled up inside me. "Look at my face!" I screamed at him. The force of my own voice surprised me. "You don't understand," I said, struggling to control myself. "I'm nineteen years old and I have to live the rest of my life like this. What am I going to do?"

CHAPTER ONE

Boy Meets World

Just two months after my mother, Maria Felix Zavala, a four-foot, eleven-inch firebrand of a woman, arrived in Texas in 1982, she met a man named Jose Martinez. He swept her off her feet with all the promises of love.

Maria was an illegal immigrant from El Salvador with no money and no English. She had chanced everything to come to the United States to make a better life. She had scraped and borrowed the funds to pay the coyote to bring her first across the borders of Guatemala and Mexico and then into America, risking her life crossing a raging river she could not swim and dodging the immigration agents who waited for people just like her. But worst of all, she had left behind in the care of her mother two young daughters, Consuelo and little Anabel, who had been born with no bones in her feet. Since Anabel couldn't walk, my mom was determined to prosper in the United States so she'd be able to buy her daughter a wheelchair.

Jose was from Monterrey, Mexico, but he'd been in the United States for a while and spoke English well. Like Maria, he was also quite short, but he was tall in attitude and had long, curly hair and straight white teeth.

Maria was working for a woman taking care of her three young children while the woman was at work. Someone whispered to Maria that the woman was a prostitute. Maria didn't really care what her employer did for a living, but the fact that she'd never paid Maria for her work was a big problem. So when Jose impulsively invited Maria to move in with him and his family, it seemed like a godsend.

"I'll take care of you," he said.

She quit her job and settled in with her new family. Unfortunately, her new mother-in-law didn't like Maria: She wanted a virgin for her son, and she knew Maria already had two children back in El Salvador. Maria tried to ignore the negativity because she wanted to be happy.

But Jose had trouble keeping jobs, and money quickly became an issue. He wasn't going to take care of her after all.

And then Maria found herself pregnant. She was determined not to let anything hold her back, so she got a job taking care of a two-year-old boy and cleaning his parents' house for eighty dollars a week. She scrubbed the toilets, swept and mopped the floors, and washed and ironed the clothes, all while chasing the busy toddler.

Little by little she managed to save a few dollars, and by December 1982 she'd begun to send some money back to her mother for the care of her daughters. As the months went by and her belly expanded, Maria worried about the stability of her relationship and speculated about whether Jose would be a responsible father. Or if he'd even be around for his child.

"It doesn't matter," she convinced herself. "I'm going to work hard. I'm going to raise my children real good."

One day Jose disappeared without a word. Three days passed before he bothered to call.

"I'm in Shreveport," he said. He had two jobs there in Louisiana, construction and restaurant work. "In a couple of weeks, I'll come back and get you. We're going to start a new life together!"

He was true to his word. The couple settled in northwest Louisiana in a town called Bossier City, along the east bank of the Red River across from Shreveport. A growing city of about fifty thousand people, it was home to several riverboat casinos as well as Harrah's Louisiana Downs, a Thorough-bred and quarter horse racetrack. There were ample service-sector jobs, but Maria was six months pregnant by then. No one would hire a woman in that condition, so she sat in the couple's apartment for months, watching Jose come and go and feeling more and more distant from him.

He seemed to prefer killing time with people whom Maria considered "good-for-nothings" instead of working. He earned a license to operate semitrailer trucks, telling Maria, "Now all I have to do is get a trucking job and we'll have it made." It didn't happen.

The atmosphere grew tense. One evening, the two were in the bedroom, arguing. Jose had had a bit to drink. He kicked Maria in the leg, and she fell, crying.

"I hope you lose that fucking baby," he said.

But she didn't.

On June 14, 1983, she gave birth to me at the LSU Medical Center in Shreveport. A snapshot from that day shows me in the arms of my smiling parents. You'd never know what my father had wished upon me just a few weeks earlier.

It's Latin American tradition to observe a period of *cuarentena*, or quarantine, for forty days after the birth of a baby. New mothers recuperate and receive special care from other women, especially another mother or a mother figure, while they bond with their babies. But this was America, and the notion of *cuarentena* was a dated fancy for a woman in my mother's circumstances.

Two weeks after I was born, my mother handed her bundle to the neighborhood babysitter. Struggling to control her roiling postpartum emotions, she forced herself to turn and walk away. Each day for eight hours my mom pushed a vacuum, hauled trash, and scrubbed toilet bowls in offices in Bossier City. By the time she returned home to me, her breasts would be heavy and aching, her back would throb, and she'd wonder how she could leave me again the next day.

When she'd cry at work, heartbroken, her coworkers would look at her irritably. "You just had a baby," they'd say. "It's not like you're going to die."

She kept working and my father kept working, and I grew into a chubby, smiling infant. The three of us were a little family unit, struggling but making it. Until we weren't.

One day my father was grumbling about my mom to one of her girlfriends.

"If you leave her, you'll have to pay child support," she told him.

"I'll go back to Mexico before I give her a dime," he replied.

In March 1984, when I was nine months old, my father vanished again. This time two weeks passed before my mom heard anything. A neighbor came to our apartment with a letter from Jose. He wrote that he wanted us to join him in his new town, DeLand, Florida, about halfway between Orlando and Daytona Beach. There, in what was sometimes called the Athens of Florida, we could be a family again.

The neighbor offered to help my mom pack up,

but her trust in Jose already was frayed. The man she'd come to know was not dependable, and she wasn't willing to go out into the great unknown without some security.

"If he wants us, he can come get us," she said.

She wrote back to him, telling him what he needed to do to bring our family together. The post office returned the letter: undeliverable as addressed. She tried more than once to send it, and then she kept it for a long time as a reminder. Someday she wanted to be able to show me why I don't have a father.

So there she was again: all alone with a baby in her arms—in addition to no papers, no car, no English, and no money. Her oldest brother had recently made it to Shreveport, so we moved in with him for a month, but my uncle was a mean drunk, "a macho man." But as long as she was able to pay for my diapers and milk, she considered it a good day.

Then my mom met the lady she calls her guardian angel, my godmother, Alejandra.

Catholic parents are expected to have their children baptized within months of birth, and my parents were obligated to designate godparents, or *padrino*s, for me. But my mom didn't know anyone in Louisiana, so I was eleven months old before she was able to bring together my *padrino*s. Her method was pretty unconventional: At Jose's work she had met a nice man named

Lupe who offered to serve as my godfather. He told my mom he'd bring along his girlfriend to the church for the baptism, and she could serve as godmother. Enter Alejandra into our lives.

Once she learned about our situation, Alejandra invited us to crowd into her little house, even though she had five kids of her own. Alejandra helped my mom land a job cleaning tables and serving chips at a Mexican restaurant. She'd work from 9 a.m. until 2 p.m. and then report back at 5 p.m., frequently working until midnight. She paid Alejandra's thirteen-year-old daughter forty dollars a week to watch me.

In the meantime, my mom had become involved with a Salvadoran guy named Miguel, a friend of her brother's. Always practical, she appreciated that he spoke English and could drive—she couldn't do either yet. Once I began to talk, I started to call him "Daddy." After four months at Alejandra's, we moved in with him and made our home there for several years. Miguel and my mom parted company because, she says, although he was a good man, he didn't have any dreams. I don't really remember anything about him.

But despite the hardships and setbacks we endured, my mom's pride remained intact. My mom dressed me up in the best clothes she could afford from the dollar store. One evening after her shift, she picked me up at Alejandra's, where Alejandra and her kids still looked after me.

Alejandra handed her one of my shirts; her husband had cut it into shreds with scissors because, Alejandra said, "It's ugly. He's a beautiful child. How can you dress him like that?"

My mom was outraged. She yanked me away and told Alejandra that they were through.

A waitress at the restaurant where my mom worked had an elderly mother everyone called Miss Mary, and she agreed to babysit me. But it soon became apparent that Miss Mary didn't have the energy to look after a toddler. I became depressed because I missed Alejandra's family. My mom was sad, too. She and Alejandra made up, and the babysitting arrangement went back to the way it had been.

It was so good for me to be back in that house. I loved to follow Alejandra's kids around and play with them. I never stopped moving. Everyone called me Nay-Nay—short for Rene—and at Alejandra's place, little Nay-Nay was the center of attention. I ate it up. I was born to be an entertainer, an *artista*. My mom says that when I would cry, all she had to do to get me to stop was pick up a camera and point it at me, and I was instantly all smiles.

I was an especially tireless talker. If I was at home with my mom or we were on the bus going somewhere, I'd start chattering. "Mom, what's that? Why do they have that there?" Talk, talk, talk, questions and more questions. My mom says

I talked as though I already knew everything. She thanked God that she wouldn't have to fight to keep me in school as she may have had to do in El Salvador.

But her undocumented status nagged at her, weighing her down with an extra layer of worry. The United States follows the English common-law rule of "right of soil": If you're born here, you're a citizen. Since I was an American, my mom considered herself the same. But Uncle Sam did not.

"La Migra"—the immigration agents—seized my mom the first time in 1985, when I was two years old. My mom was busy at work, helping the cook make the platters of tacos and enchiladas and setting up for happy hour. The next thing she knew, agents had lined up her and her coworkers against a wall.

"Where are your papers?" the agents demanded, going down the row of undocu-mented employees —several Mexicans and two Salvadorans. My mom was the sole woman. A few of the workers attempted to argue their way out of this jam, but that didn't work.

My mom burst into tears as the agents herded her and the other employees into a van. "Please, I have a son!" she cried through the wire separator.

At the immigration office, they booked all the men, but they told my mom she could go. Plane tickets to El Salvador were expensive, they said, so she needed to save her money to buy her own. "Come back to the office in three months with the funds," they told her. "We'll help you get home."

It wasn't clear if they were giving her a break because she was the lone woman, because she had a child, or because the cost of the ticket really was the issue, but she'd take it any way it came. She wasn't ready to give up her American dream.

By this time she had found very steady employment. She worked at her first job of the day, the Mexican restaurant, from 9 a.m. to 2 p.m. Later in the afternoon she reported to her job as a kitchen helper at the Italian Garden, a Bossier City restaurant. She worked there until eleven o'clock or midnight—a job she kept for years.

The Italian Garden was a great place to work. The owners, Frank and his wife, Jan, were very good to my mother, and her coworkers had begun to feel like family. Once in a while I'd hang out in the empty banquet room, and by the time I was about six years old sometimes I'd even help the servers bring meals and drinks out to the tables. At closing time, I'd wash down the kitchen mats with a hose. I loved it.

At the same time, my mom had been working toward getting American citizenship. She'd contacted a New Orleans lawyer who was supposed to be able to help immigrants successfully apply for green cards. About once a month, she and I would take a five-hour bus ride to the city to check on her application. She had paid the lawyer several hundred dollars of her diligently saved money, and then she'd waited, and waited, and waited.

Meanwhile, throughout her time in the States, my mom was haunted by the guilt of leaving her girls back in El Salvador. From the time I was very little, I sensed that I was keeping my mom away from my sisters, a feeling that was compounded on the rare occasions when my mom would become frustrated and lash out at me about our situation. But I didn't have her, either, really, since she was always working.

This guilt, combined with the lack of progress on her green card, sapped her willpower and finally did her in. Her brother was planning a trip back home in April 1987. My mom decided that we would go back too—for good. She would finally put her conscience to rest and rid herself of the constant specter of potential deportation.

She called Frank at the restaurant. "I'm not coming in anymore," she told him. "I'm finished with this place."

"Don't leave," he said. "This is Nay-Nay's country. If you go, he won't have the opportunities he'll have here."

Frank called the lawyer and told him my mom was planning to leave. The lawyer got on the phone with her right away and echoed Frank's pleas to her.

My mom looked over at me playing with my toys. She pictured me grown up, speaking fluent English, enjoying the possibilities America would offer me.

Okay, then, she thought. *One day I'll become legal and bring my girls here, too.* She unpacked the suitcases.

She'd bought two identical pink ruffled dresses to take to my sisters in El Salvador. She sent the dresses to her brother and asked him to deliver them for her. At least her girls would have a little piece of her and know she hadn't forgotten them. But one of my sisters never got the chance to wear her dress.

A few days later, my mom got a call from a cousin in El Salvador. It was the sort of call no mother should ever have to take. Her baby girl Anabel, just six years old, was dead.

My mom stood with the phone to her ear, not speaking.

"Are you there? Are you there?" her cousin asked.

Finally my mom summoned the will to speak, if only one word: "How?"

Her cousin explained that Anabel had burned with a fever for several days. In their little village, an illness that might be cured easily with a dose of antibiotics often ushered in death.

"We fixed her up real nice for the burial, Maria. She's an angel now."

My mom continued to listen in silence as her cousin pressed on.

"There's nothing you can do now."

My mom felt something heavy on her chest and she couldn't draw enough breath. She hung up.

Although I was not even four years old, I hugged and kissed her and told her it would be okay. My mom didn't want to move away from the phone because she thought that maybe—just maybe—her family had been playing a terrible joke on her. Maybe her cousin was only kidding. She waited by the phone all day for another phone call, but it never came.

For days afterward, my mom couldn't get out of bed. Frank and Jan begged her to come back to work until finally she did. She didn't want to, but she knew she had to. She needed to buy our food, make our rent.

My sister's death made my mom realize that America—with all its advantages—really was the best place for us now, although she still missed my sister Consuelo terribly.

CHAPTER TWO

American Dreams

We settled into a comfortable routine of school and work. My mom was so proud when I marched off to my first day of kindergarten at Waller Elementary School. I didn't speak much English yet, but she promised herself that as soon as I began to learn it in school, we'd speak it at home together.

In February 1988, La Migra appeared again, this time at the Mexican restaurant where everyone except my mom was legal.

"Put on my coat and go sit at a table like you're a customer," a coworker urged. My mom refused. She felt like she'd already spent enough time in the shadows. She was proud of who she was and all she'd endured to forge a life in this country. She believed that she deserved to be here. But if La Migra deported her, she'd take me back to the old country, knowing that at least with my own papers in hand I could return when I was eighteen.

The officers cuffed her and put her in their van. On the way to the immigration office, she said,

"Please, I need to pick up my son from day care."

The two men conferred quietly. She couldn't hear what they were saying. And then, to her surprise, they pulled over.

"Get out," one of the agents said. "We know something's going on at your restaurant. We know people are selling drugs. We'll come back and see you soon, and you can tell us what you know."

My mom didn't know anything about drugs. What she did know was that she needed to find a new daytime job. It didn't make any sense to be there waiting when La Migra came back.

The years of hiding and fear finally ended in December 1988, when the New Orleans lawyer came through—my mom received her green card. She was a legal worker. Our fridge may have been empty because she'd spent all our money on the immigration process, but she didn't care. She cried with happiness, which she'd never done before. I can't imagine the relief she felt, the weight of all that worry finally lifted from her shoulders. (Five years later she applied for U.S. citizenship, and in March 1999 she received her American flag.)

My mother's legal status also meant we were free to travel to El Salvador. I was just six years old the first time. My Spanish wasn't so great once I'd started learning English in school, and I think my mom was a little bit embarrassed. In her mind, my weak language skills reflected poorly on her among her kin.

When we arrived in the capital, San Salvador, we caught a bus to my mom's hometown. But the bus went only as far as the town center; from there we had to go by horseback to her mother's home. I found it tremendously exciting. I'd never been near a horse before, but I confidently rode ahead of everyone else. At the home I met my grandmother, aunts, uncles, cousins, and my half sister, Consuelo, who was about twelve years old.

I'd said hi to her on the phone a few times, but I was thrilled to meet her in person. We got along really well and immediately began to behave like a typical brother and sister despite our language barrier. I'd push open the door when she was in her room getting dressed, and she'd retaliate by chasing me around the house and hitting me.

The El Salvador culture was full of surprises. I thought it was fun to go to the bathroom in the forest, although I was slightly embarrassed and always made sure no one saw me wander away to do my business. No bathtubs or showers? Even better. What boy wants to bathe? If we had to do it, there was always the creek.

One time I saw a kid, maybe a few years older than me, carrying a machete. A couple of days later, I saw another boy who also had one. I was confused: Why did I have to play with toy weapons but these kids were allowed to have real ones? Like many boys, I was fascinated by guns and dangerous things.

My grandmother had kept the dress that my mom had sent for Anabel two years earlier. Now she asked to have it back, but my grandmother refused, saying she wanted to be buried with it. My mom and I returned home without it.

My mom wouldn't get it back for two more years. During another visit to El Salvador, she again asked for the dress. She told my grandmother it would make her feel better, feel closer to Anabel. My grandmother agreed to let it go back to the United States under the condition that the person who dies first—my grandmother or my mom—gets buried with it.

My mother's legal status brought her much-needed relief, even happiness, but for me, it didn't make that much difference. Not because I didn't care, but because I was already a happy kid. I knew my mom struggled sometimes, but she always managed to keep my world safe and untroubled, and I never had any reason to believe my life was harder than or different from the lives of other kids.

Except for not having a father. By the time I was in the first or second grade, I realized I'd been missing a man in my life. I'd see dads come to pick up their kids at school, coach their sons on the football field. If I had a dad, I thought, he could play catch with me. Instead, I had to throw a ball up on the roof and play catch by myself.

And then my mom met Hector. I was eight years old.

Monday was the one day a week my mom had off from her job at the Italian Garden. She'd gone to a club for a rare night out—to listen to music, dance a little *cumbia* in her white dress and heels —and there was Hector. Good-looking and educated—he'd been a teacher in Mexico— Hector was studying computers here in the United States. They started dating, and pretty quickly my mom was hooked.

While Hector was around, I had a dad. He was the first man who made me understand what a father could be. Hector could be strict with me, but I knew it was because he didn't want some kid pulling one over on him. He wanted to spend time with me. He taught me how to change the oil in a car, showing me how to slide beneath the engine of our green Ford Escort, loosen the screws, and drain the oil. I'd help him pour the fluid through to clean out the system and then replace the filter.

He roughhoused and wrestled with me a lot. He'd be walking past nonchalantly and suddenly reach out and punch me in the arm. "Got ya!" he'd say.

I'd laugh, and then I'd chase him so I could punch him in the arm, too. He'd pretend I'd hit him hard and he'd go down. Then we'd both die laughing.

Hector also taught me to love music. He set up a keyboard in our apartment. He'd place his ashtray on the keyboard, gesture for me to sit beside him on the bench. I'd take the cigarette from his mouth and put it into the ashtray for him, and we'd sing Spanish love songs together. He had a beautiful tenor voice. He was tough and gentle at the same time, and I totally respected that.

Sometimes we would walk down the street from our apartment to a bar called JC's, where Hector played keyboards and I put on a little show. I'd dance the *cumbia*, and I'd sing tender songs about broken hearts filled with pain. It was during these evenings that I realized I loved being in front of people, making them happy. It made me feel good about myself.

But then Hector started hitting my mom, and it was hard for me to reconcile that violence with the man I was trying to love. His way was all I knew, but I knew enough to understand that it was wrong.

The first time it happened I was inside our apartment playing a video game. Out of the blue I heard my mom scream. I ran outside and saw my mom bent back against the hood of the car, Hector leaning over her, his arm drawn with a clenched fist. Before I had a moment to react, he punched her in the face.

"Get in the house!" my mom screamed at me.

I obeyed, and at that moment I loved her even harder than I already did. I sat in the back of the closet, hugging my knees, afraid to make a sound. *That's my mom and he's hurting her!* my nine-year-old mind screamed. *Is he going to kill her?* Soon enough it was over. But it was not an isolated incident. When Hector drank, all bets were off. One day, the three of us went to visit some friends at a barbecue. Hector boozed pretty heavily at the party. My mom got fed up and insisted we leave.

When we got back to our place, she and I went in but Hector stayed outside. The door had barely closed behind us when we heard the sound of shattering glass. My mom went out and discovered that Hector had smashed a beer bottle in the driveway. He was in a rage. He began yelling at her and soon had her pinned down, roaring in her face.

I ran out and jumped on his back. "Please, Daddy, don't hurt my mama!"

In one swift motion, he shrugged me off him, turned to face me, and slapped me across the face so hard I spun around. It was the first time he'd ever hit me.

"Rene, go call the police!" my mom managed to sputter.

I didn't get the chance. Hector grabbed both of us by the hair.

"Shut your faces! I should fucking kill you!"

He began marching us to the railroad tracks near our apartment. He laid us across the tracks and held us down by our throats. I began to cough hard, which seemed to anger him even more.

"Shut up, you little brat," he spit. "I could choke you to death."

My mom is petite, not even five feet tall, and I was only a little boy. We were no match for Hector.

But then, inexplicably, he changed his mind and let us up.

"Get in the car," he barked. "We're going to my place."

It was a long drive to his house, which was located deep in the woods. Who knew what he was going to do with us there?

On the way, Hector's thirst got the better of him and he stopped to buy more beer.

While he was in the store, I leaned over the front seat to ask my mom, "What now?"

"The first chance you see to make a run for it, you get away and call the police," she whispered, without turning her head.

I was ready to bolt right then, but Hector was already on his way back to the car, a six-pack under his arm. He opened a can and took a big gulp before starting the engine.

We were driving down a dark lane alongside the Red River when Hector suddenly stopped in the middle of the road. I was terrified.

"You be quiet, Rene," my mom said over her

shoulder to me in the backseat. No doubt she thought if I cried or said anything, I might provoke Hector. I kept my mouth shut.

"Get out," Hector ordered. My mom opened the front passenger door, while I pulled on the latch on the door in back. Hector didn't move. When I looked back into the car from the side of the road, Hector's hands were still on the steering wheel. He leaned forward, his forehead resting on his knuckles.

"Fuck this. Get back in. I'll take you home."

Maybe his rage had burned out. Or maybe his beer fog lifted just enough for him to come to his senses about what he was doing to these two people who loved him. We'll never know.

When we pulled into the parking lot by our apartment, I saw my chance.

"I have to pee."

"So go pee," he said. He and my mother stayed in the car.

I walked inside and dialed 911. Within minutes, I heard the sirens come screeching into the lot. I went outside in time to watch the police officers cuffing Hector. My mom ran to my side.

"When I get out, I'm going to kill you!" he screamed at us. His finger impressions were still visible on my face.

I was furious that he was trying to hurt us, to hurt my mom. There had been incidents before this, when they had fought and I'd wished I could do something, clenching my little fists and growling in frustration. I wasn't just angry at him then, but her, too. Why was she letting this happen? I knew she needed a man in her life, an adult relationship, but why was she putting herself through this? Why was she putting *me* through this?

CHAPTER THREE

Hope

My mother bought a gun off a guy on the street, and he showed her how to use it. "Don't shoot him in the back, or you'll get in trouble," he told her. "And don't kill him—just shoot him in the leg."

I didn't know anything about the gun, and thankfully my mom never needed to use it, but Hector's threat was never far from her thoughts. It seemed like a good time for a fresh start.

My uncle had moved to Hope, Arkansas, the previous summer, so we picked up and followed him. Although my mom fielded some initial resistance from me about the move, I had to admit that the name seemed promising.

Nestled in the rural southwest part of the state, Hope was the epitome of small-town living, but it was starting to get national recognition as the birthplace of Bill Clinton, who was then campaigning to become our forty-second president. He touted the town in his 1992 nomination acceptance speech when he said, "I still believe in a place called Hope."

I don't know what Hope was like back when he lived there, but our experience wasn't quite so idyllic. Home to about ten thousand residents, Hope didn't support many high-paying jobs, but there were ample factory positions that offered steady paychecks. My uncle helped my mom land a job in quality control at a chicken-processing plant located in an industrial park on one side of town. The pay was good—nine dollars an hour—but her schedule was lousy. Assigned to the graveyard shift, she left for the plant every night at around nine thirty, not returning home until eight thirty or nine the next morning. That meant every evening she'd put me to bed and head out for work, leaving me alone in our duplex apartment all night. I was nine years old.

Most of the time, being left alone didn't bother me. The only time I got scared was late at night when I couldn't sleep. I loved to watch cop or mystery shows, but when I settled down in front of the TV, the only light in the darkened living room came in an eerie glow from the set, casting shadows on the walls. Sometimes I got spooked, convinced I heard a strange noise from somewhere in the apartment. Fear would march up my spine like a line of fire ants, and I'd crawl under the table in the living room to hide, wondering if someone was watching me through a window. Fortunately, that didn't happen too often.

My mom worked six days a week, off only on

Sundays, so I was pretty much in charge of myself. Every school day I'd get myself up and dressed. I'd eat ham and cheese Hot Pockets or Cinnamon Toast Crunch for breakfast before heading out to catch the school bus to William J. Clinton Primary School, where I attended the third grade. If I had some change and left early enough, I'd stop at the ramshackle market next door to our apartment and buy myself a honey bun and a Yoo-hoo.

After school let out in the afternoon, I'd ride the bus home. From the bus stop I'd walk straight to the store and buy myself a twenty-ounce Dr Pepper and a bag of Doritos. I relished my independence and felt proud that I could take care of myself.

These were the days before after-school programs, so I was one of the millions of America's "latchkey kids" who returned from school to an empty home. I kept our key in my pocket, and its weight against my leg comforted me. My mom didn't know about the research that said that kids left unsupervised for long periods of time often experienced behavioral problems and lower levels of self-esteem, but she sure as hell wasn't going to let me get into trouble if she could help it. She didn't hesitate to dole out swift and decisive punishment when I got out of line.

That was at home. At school, where I was out of her reach, I got into a lot of trouble defending myself on the playground because kids picked on me for all the reasons kids can find to pick on someone: I was the new boy. I had a Louisiana accent. My name was Rene, which sounded like a girl's name. I kind of looked like a girl, with long hair and silky skin. (Later, in high school, girls would ask me if my mom worked on my eyebrows because they were so clean.)

The first fight I ever got into was in the fourth grade, with a kid called A.J. It seemed like he called everyone in the class "cousin," which bugged me. *He sure has a lot of relatives,* I thought. On this particular day, the teacher stepped out of the classroom, and A.J. started in on a couple of other students. He'd been teasing me all year, and when he turned his attention in my direction, something just went off in me. I jumped out of my chair and told him to step up. We faced off nose to nose, and I gave him a push. He shoved me back. We spent the next few seconds in a standoff, and then I took a swing, and we began to roll around. I felt victorious right up until I was marched to the principal's office. My mom was going to kill me.

Over the next few years, my mom would get a lot of calls about me. At first kids had picked on me because I was new. But they kept ganging up on me for any reason at all, especially on the school bus. I fought back. But that meant my exhausted mom would walk through the door from work in the morning only to receive a phone call summoning her to school because I'd gotten into trouble again. The principal finally asked her if school administrators could paddle me when I acted up instead of calling her to come in. She agreed.

Many parents advocated corporal punishment for their children, and Arkansas was one of a handful of states where it was avidly practiced. Children were offered a choice of disciplinary methods: a detention, an out-of-school suspension, or a paddling—two or three hard whacks with a board—often called "licks."

I hated being paddled, of course, and it didn't teach me a thing. It seemed to happen to me on a weekly basis through the fifth grade. Every time, I'd walk out of the principal's office the same as I went in: defiant and angry but newly determined not to ruin my mom's sanity with my poor behavior.

At home my mom was able to exercise more control over me. She didn't want me to leave the apartment when she was at work or sleeping off her shift, so I spent my afternoons and evenings watching TV and playing Super Mario Bros. She'd usually sleep on the couch in the living room so she'd hear me if I tried to sneak out. But sometimes I got past her anyway. Her long shifts at the plant were draining, so she slept pretty hard. And I knew what time she usually woke up, so I would make sure I was back inside well before then. If I got my clothes dirty while I was playing outside, I'd have to hide them until wash day.

Every so often, though, I'd get nailed. When that happened, she'd tear a switch off a tree and come after me. Imagine a nine- or ten-year-old crying and running down the street from his mom. It was so embarrassing. She couldn't catch me, but eventually I had to return home, and that's when it would get really ugly. I'd try to stay out of her way back at the apartment, but inside she was able to catch me. I'd hold my hands over my butt to cushion the blows.

Afterward, she'd always come back to make up with me and try to explain why she'd punished me. "I love you very much, mijo, and I want you to do well in life. You have to listen to me. I'm your mother."

Still, I felt sad when I'd look out the window at my friends playing in the apartment parking lot. If someone outside would fall or do something funny, I'd laugh out loud. If my mom was awake, I'd stand in front of the door and sigh loudly, hoping she'd get the hint that I wanted to go out. If that didn't work, I'd have myself a good long pout.

Sometimes my friends noticed me watching them from the window. I'd signal them to knock on the door, hoping they might have some luck with my mom. I'd strategically place myself out of range of the door so my mom wouldn't think I'd had anything to do with the plan. And sometimes she said yes when one of my friends asked, "Can Jose come out and play?"

Actually, over the years friends had been a bit hard to come by. I was one of the very few Latino kids in a largely African-American community. It was a relief when I met Juan Bautista when we were sixth graders at Beryl Henry Upper Elementary School. Juan was born in the United States, but he had lived most of his life in Mexico, where his dad, a preacher, had a congregation. Juan didn't speak English, and the other students picked on him, yelling things like "Go back to Mexico!"

As two of only five Hispanic kids in our class, Juan and I eventually became allies. Juan—or Mucho, as he was called—was used to getting beaten up, but once we became friends, I became his protector. I knew how it felt to be isolated and teased.

Around this time, my mom met Sergio, a slight Mexican man. From the very beginning I wasn't a fan. Sergio slouched like a question mark and smacked his lips when he ate. He was mostly bald with a few sparse threads of long black hair sprouting east and west. What I disliked most was that he was loud, always saying things he thought were hilarious but I didn't find funny at all.

But my mom was still getting over Hector, and she really wanted us to be part of a family, so it wasn't long before she and Sergio got married and we moved into his house. The two of us never clicked, although I tried hard to keep my feelings from my mother. But I was delighted when, only eight months later, my mom told me they were splitting up. I guess they didn't click much, either.

She and I moved into a trailer home, and once again it was just the two of us.

Financially, we were a big family. My mom wasn't just supporting the two of us on her salary: She was still sending a monthly allowance to support my sister and grandmother in El Salvador. "Overtime" was her middle name.

My mom was open with me about our finances. She'd show me her paycheck and we'd look at the bills together. That way I'd see with my own eyes what was left over. It made me feel like I understood our situation. She always made sure I had five outfits, one for every day of the school week, because she didn't want me to get teased for wearing the same clothes.

If there were things that we wanted beyond the basics, we'd shop at stores where we could put stuff on layaway. I never tried to push my mom into buying something we couldn't afford, but if we had the cash, she'd lay it out for me. She didn't say no to me very often, and if she did, she'd explain that she didn't have the money at the moment but that once she'd saved it, we'd return for the item.

Once, though, my desire for something we couldn't afford got the better of me. I was obsessed for a short time with pencils decorated with NFL logos. A store called Fred's sold packs of them for a couple of bucks apiece. One day when I was there with my mom, I decided to steal some. I knew it was wrong, but I snuck away and, with my heart pounding, I opened up a package of these pencils and stuffed some into my waistband. Who would look down a kid's pants for stolen merchandise?

It was a great plan, until those pencils began to work their way down my pants leg as I walked through the store. Finally they dropped out. A store employee grabbed me and marched me over to my mom. She was angry, I was ashamed, and it only took this one instance to demonstrate to me that stealing wasn't the way to get the things you wanted. I vowed to myself that as soon as I was old enough, I'd get a job to help my mother with the bills and earn the things I wanted instead of taking them.

But it wasn't all virtue that motivated me. I had recently discovered the very best reason to have a little bit of spending money in your pocket—girls.

My mom warned me about them.

"Be careful," she said. "They might trick you. Don't fall into their trap."

"No, Mama, I won't," I'd assure her.

Even so, I got my first girlfriend at age eleven. By seventh grade, I had figured out that my looks were attracting attention. The kids at Yerger Middle School seemed to notice me before I even opened my mouth. Girls claimed to like me even if I'd never spoken to them. They'd write notes and "accidentally" drop them near me so I could read them. Our home phone would ring on Friday nights, and when I answered I'd get an earful of anonymous giggling on the other end. Even my buddies joined in, dutifully relaying messages that this girl or that one liked me. I recognized this as an asset, so I began to work very hard on cultivating my pretty-boy image.

One day I was standing in the cafeteria at lunch, talking with a girl. I liked her, but she was looking at someone else.

"Wow," she said, flicking a glance at a kid walking by. "He looks good."

"What's so hot about him?" I asked. He looked pretty ordinary to me.

"He looks more mature," she answered. "Clean."

That's all she said, but it got me thinking. I decided to start taking care of myself. Every morning I painstakingly ironed my jeans so they had a sharp crease down the middle of each leg. I would pair them with a Ralph Lauren or Nautica polo shirt in aqua or yellow. And then to top it off, a spray of my cologne, Cool Water. Giving myself a final inspection in the bathroom mirror, I'd spritz on a little more for the finishing touch. Not bad for a twelve-year-old.

For me, it was all about attention and being "that guy," the guy everyone watched. Looking back, I think that craving had a lot to do with how lonely I was. My mom did her best, but since it was just the two of us and her hours were so crazy, I missed having someone around to keep me company—a brother or sister, a father, a grand-parent. Hell, even a dog would've been great.

So I approached looking good and being popu-lar like it was a part-time job. At school I'd rush to the bathroom at every break to put a little water on my hands and touch them to my hair to keep the shine. Then I would stand there on a corner of the campus, prop up a leg, and talk to my friends. Girls would walk by and smile. I'd grin back.

I didn't realize those ambitions were hollow, and that someday they would all go up in smoke. I even fantasized about what it'd be like to get into an accident so I could find out how many people really cared. Maybe a strange thought for a kid and interesting in its prophecy.

"Be careful who you surround yourself with," my mom would remind me. "Everyone is your friend on the surface, but only a few are your friend at the root. People will come into your life and say all the right things, but you must be cautious."

It was as if she had a crystal ball.

Sometimes my efforts backfired. Certain girls would develop a crush on me, but if I didn't respond in kind this inspired hurt feelings. A couple of times these girls would ask an older brother or cousin for help.

I usually walked home from school with a bunch of my friends, but since my place was the farthest away, I walked the last four or five blocks alone. One afternoon I was strolling along when a group of older guys approached me.

"Hey," one of them said. "I hear you think you're too good for my cousin."

I couldn't believe it: I was going to get my ass kicked by grown men just because I didn't want to date their cousin. I hurried away without responding. After that, I started taking a different route home.

But soon enough they ambushed me. There were three of them in a car, and they drove up next to me.

"Hey, punk!" they shouted. "Remember us?"

I put my head down and kept on walking.

"Don't you hear us talking to you?"

They hopped out and surrounded me, pushing me back and forth like a pinball. Then they began to punch me. They knocked me down, and I curled into a ball, my backpack facing upward like a turtle shell.

When they finally stopped, I jumped up and

ran the rest of the way home. I didn't tell my mom what had happened, but in no time she extracted the story. As usual, she had a suggestion for me.

"What do you think a tiger does when he gets chased and cornered?" she asked me. If I was ever threatened or in danger, she said, I needed to fight back if I wanted to survive.

CHAPTER FOUR

Football Dreams

I was only ten years old when I played my first football game with a neighborhood team in Hope. I had been introduced to the great game of football by Alejandra's three sons back in Bossier City before we moved. It had been a huge thrill when the boys let me grab the ball and run from them. It was enough to fuel my appetite for the game, despite the fact that other kids were bigger and faster.

When I finally joined the team in Hope in fifth grade, I didn't have any clue about the rules beyond tackling, blocking, and scoring. I couldn't have cared less where the coach put me as long as I was on the field. What I couldn't know then was that the major elements of the game—strategy, tactics, exploiting the opponents' weaknesses, and gaining territory—were skills that would come to mean life or death to me years later.

During my second game, I found myself face-to-face with a behemoth player on the opposing team. He was the same age as me, but he looked like he'd already conquered puberty. Hell, he looked like he could probably drive *and* vote. He ran the ball. My position was safety, sometimes considered the most challenging spot on the defense side. It was my job to stop him, but I was afraid to get in his way.

In the game's last moments, our coach yelled for a time-out.

"Listen up, team. I don't care if you don't want to hit this guy. You have to give it a try!"

He looked straight at me. I gulped.

We broke from the huddle. During the next play, the giant ran down the sideline right at me. I was the only obstacle between him and the end zone. *It's now or never,* I thought. I dove right into him and knocked him down. I couldn't believe I'd done it. I bounced up in celebration, ignoring how much that tackle had actually hurt.

From that moment, I knew I wanted to play this game forever. The admiration I saw in the other kids' eyes was a kind of validation I hadn't previously experienced. The inherent physicality of the game indulged the rough, tough, edgy side of me. Perhaps most important, it made me part of something, when I'd never been a part of anything before.

By the time I started at Hope High School, I had visions of football stardom dancing in my head. Our team, the Bobcats, led by head coach Kevin Stamp and assistant coach Gene Stubber, had a great record.

Trouble was, I was still kind of small for a football player. Practice after practice, it seemed my role was just to serve as a tackling dummy for the bigger and more talented players. During games, I barely set foot on the field unless our team was winning big. Initially, that didn't bother me; all I really cared about was being part of this team.

Maybe a little too much. I started fooling around in the classroom, getting into trouble again. After practice I stopped going straight home as my mom expected. My mom really didn't get the allure of football or understand the rules. She called it "a game where a bunch of chickens with their heads cut off run after a ball." So if I wasn't going to do what I was supposed to do, she was going to take it away.

She called Coach Stubber, a veteran educator and a laid-back country guy, and told him she was going to remove me from the team. Luckily, Coach thought I was the kind of person who could focus when I needed to, that I wasn't just a cutup. By taking away football, my mom would create a vacuum of free time for me which, he pointed out to her, could beget even bigger problems. Coach told her he'd try to wear me out at practice so I wouldn't have energy to get into trouble. I might just go home and tend to my homework and my chores.

Even though she thought the game was silly,

she understood how much it meant to me and took Coach's words to heart. She allowed me to continue playing. Every afternoon I'd go to practice, get pummeled, and go home, bruised and aching. I had never felt such complete happiness. And to her credit, whenever she could, my mom was in the bleachers for my games, clapping, throwing her arms in the air, screaming my name.

As a sophomore I managed to gain a toehold on the field. I'd grown a little and learned a lot about the game, and the coaches seemed a little more amenable to subbing me in. I loved the challenge of stepping up and making the play, winning the praise of the head coach, Kevin Stamp.

Coach Stamp always wore a baseball cap and the kind of short-shorts that would make you cringe today. He had an extra-strong but indistinguishable accent and an ever-present wad of snuff in his cheek. I managed to become one of his favorites by finding ways to catch his attention via my play both on the field and off. I was the jokester: clowning around, messing with the other players, playing pranks. He got a kick out of it when we'd mock his accent.

My two best friends, Jacob and Jeris, were Caucasian and African-American, so Stamp and Stubber began to call the three of us "the Multicultural Idiots." They thought that was pretty funny.

Around the middle of the season I was called into Coach Stamp's office. The hair bristled on the back of my neck.

"Your counselor sent me your midterm grades," he told me. "They're pretty bad."

I stared at him, clenching my jaw, wondering what was coming next.

"You won't be able to finish out the season."

It was true that I rarely studied, that I blew off homework when it was inconvenient—which was pretty much all the time, as far as I was concerned. I hadn't figured out that I needed to sustain a decent grade point average to maintain player eligibility. All that really had mattered was putting on my pads, lacing up my cleats, and practicing with my buddies.

And despite my mother's desire for me to succeed, she hadn't stressed academics, either. She'd really known only one thing in her life: work. Her own priorities were putting food on the table and a roof over our heads while keeping me safe. My mother never got to have an education and here I was taking mine for granted.

I stood in front of the coach's desk begging him to give me the chance to bring up my grades so I could continue playing. I vowed to do better. But his tone was cold, and his response never wavered. I was heartbroken.

The following Friday at school—game day—everyone asked me why I wasn't wearing my jersey. I was full of excuses, mumbling some-thing about an injury, a swollen elbow or a trick ankle. I couldn't tell the truth because I didn't want people to think I was dumb.

I felt the prickle of shame even more acutely around my mom. She was the last person I wanted to disappoint and I skirted the truth with her as well. I don't recall what lie I told her, but it was probably something along the lines of "Since I'm only a sophomore, the coach is making me sit out." Despite being banned from participating, I continued to attend the games—if only to watch from the bleachers along with the parents, siblings, and other students. Relegated to spectator status felt like an added layer of disgrace to my punishment. I couldn't let this happen to me ever again.

That winter and spring I managed to bring up my grades. In class I stopped sitting in the very last row, where the screwups congregated. I stayed after school for extra help, and I actually did my part of the work when we did group projects. I was going to get back on that team no matter what.

Although I had always been more of a role player rather than a star, I started to think earnestly about making it to the pros. I envisioned making a better life for me and my mom. I imagined other boys wearing my jersey—as I'd worn the jerseys of professional players as a kid. I was going to be the next big thing. I would make all these spectacular plays and have thousands—potentially millions—of people cheering for me.

Ever since I played my first game at ten years old, I had stoked this fantasy, and now it evolved into a goal. At that point, I never dreamed of anything else. Honestly, it's not like I had many options. Since football was something I knew, I came to believe it was my destiny.

So with visions of college and the NFL motivating me, I spent those broiling months during the summer before my junior year working out nearly every day, pumping iron and panting through wind sprints. My mother bought me a parachute to use as a training aid. I would strap it to my waist so that when I ran it caught the wind, providing resistance.

I also got my learner's permit that summer, although I'd actually had my first turn behind the wheel when I was twelve: There was a Piggly Wiggly grocery store down the street from our place, and one Sunday evening my mom needed something—an onion, maybe—as she was cooking dinner. She let me take the Dodge Caravan to the store, and I successfully maneuvered there and back. So now that I was almost a legal driver, my mom and I brokered an agreement that when she came home from work every morning, I could take her car to the high school, where I would use the gym and run the track or up and down the bleachers. Even though I was supposed to have another person in the car, a licensed driver who was over eighteen, my mom trusted me enough to ignore that rule.

On weekends my mom went with me to the high school so I could run the track as she walked it. She used a stopwatch at her job at the plant, so she'd bring it to time me as I ran, checking my progress.

I grew stronger and faster. I was doing everything I could to become the athlete I wanted to be.

That summer, I got the idea that I wanted to meet my father. I'd had moments growing up when I'd thought of him, but it was almost always in abstract, as in wouldn't it be nice to have a father to play catch with me, to teach me how to drive, to talk to me about girls? I wondered why he'd left and why he never sought me out.

One day when I was about five years old, I found the photo of my mom holding me as an infant with my father beside her. I pointed at him.

"Who's that guy?" I asked.

"That's your daddy," she told me.

"Can I talk to my daddy?" I asked.

My mom knew how to reach my dad's mother in Houston. She could call her and track down Jose.

"You want to?" my mom asked. "I'll dial for you."

I stopped her hand as it reached for the phone. I was suddenly anxious and confused. What would I say to this man, my daddy?

"No, never mind," I said. "I don't want to talk to him. I love you, Mama."

But now I wanted to make it happen. I didn't want to upset my mom, so I tried to find him myself. I called directory assistance in Houston, which was where I thought he might still live.

"You're looking for a Jose Martinez?" the operator asked me.

"Yes," I told her.

She laughed. "Which one do you want?"

I was willing to make ten or twenty calls to find the right one. "I'll take all of them," I said.

She laughed again. "Well, there are a couple thousand," she said.

Discouraged, I thanked her and hung up.

Over the years, my mom didn't hesitate to tell me stories about my dad when I'd ask her. She told me that he would hold me and I'd stop crying and fall asleep in his arms. When he ate, he'd go back for seconds and then remain standing so the food could go straight down and he wouldn't get a gut.

So I ended up asking my mom for help tracking him down after all. She wasn't happy about it, but she remembered where Jose's mother lived and agreed to make the six-hour drive to Houston with me.

When we pulled up to the door of the Houston house, my mom said, "Go knock on the door, mijo."

I felt jittery as I got out of the car. What would I say to this stranger, my father? I walked up to the door, took a deep breath, and knocked. Nothing. Nobody answered. I knocked again. An elderly woman slowly pulled open the door and her eyes rested on my face.

"Rene!" she said. I turned back to the car and waved to my mom before folding into my grandmother's arms. She motioned at my mom to come in.

I walked into the dark house and sat on the couch, and my mom followed. My grandmother asked me how I'd been. She and my mom talked a bit about the old days.

I finally interrupted them. "Abuela," I said, then switching to English. "I came here to meet my father. Do you know where he is?"

We'd missed him by a day. He had just gone, and she offered no explanation.

I felt disappointment rake my heart and I sat, numb, while my mom and grandmother chattered on.

The telephone rang and my grandmother answered it. I heard a woman's voice blare out.

"Guess who's here!" my grandmother told the caller. "Maria and Rene!"

My mom took the phone and spoke to whoever was on the other end. When she finished, she told my grandmother that we were going to head out. My grandmother left the room for a minute and when she came back she pressed a worn hundred-dollar bill into my hand. I refused— from the looks of her home, I didn't think she could spare it— but she insisted. I used that money to buy lunch for me and my mom and to put gas in the car for the drive back home, where football and my life were.

I never did meet my father.

In preseason practice one hot August afternoon, I was trying to block a senior who seemed to weigh more than two-thirds of the team. I stood before him, believing that he wasn't coming at me full force. When someone is that big, it seems unimaginable that he could travel very fast. I stepped in front of him, confident in my ability to block him. He rolled right over me like an earth-mover. It was a scene right out of a Spanish bullfight—he was the rampaging bull, and I was the fluttering cape.

I was bent over backward by the force of the blow. My ankle twisted and I heard a snap. If a dying dream could make a sound, that was it.

I fell to the ground, twisting in pain. A couple of

my teammates helped me off the field. I sat on the sidelines until practice was over, my ankle swelling to the size of a tangerine.

Hobbling into the locker room, I found Coach Stamp. I explained what had happened and showed him my inflated ankle.

"You shouldn't have stepped in front of the big man," he boomed.

Yeah, thanks, I thought, realizing that there would be no sympathy from him.

My mom took me to see an orthopedist, who told us that the tendons and ligaments were damaged; he recommended surgery. I knew surgery would mean I'd be out for weeks and I'd miss the season. All that hard work wasted. I decided to defer the operation until spring.

So I rubbed on Icy Hot gel, soaked the ankle in Epsom salts, and iced it. Again and again. My mother took me to see an acquaintance of hers who massaged my ankle to help the swelling. The massage felt good, but it didn't do a thing for the injury.

And I continued to play. As I grimaced through practices, it was clear my former speed was gone. I could barely keep up with the slowest guys out there.

The first game of the season rolled around and expectations were high for the Hope Bobcats. I was sidelined because of the injury, so I channeled my energy into pumping up the crowds. I would throw my hands in the air and flap my towel, encouraging everyone in the stands to leap up, yell louder.

Over the course of the season, I got back on the field from time to time, but the constant pain kept me from gaining much ground. The coach would roar at me: "Martinez!" and I would race over to him. "Go get the quarterback!" he'd yell. "Use your speed to rush past the blocker!" Hearing the confidence in his voice often gave me the boost I needed to run through the pain, to justify his decision to put me in. My mother was always in the stands, screaming loudly enough for me to hear her.

Invested in helping me heal in any way she could, my mom called on some folklore. In some Hispanic cultures—in Spain, Mexico, and the southwestern United States—there's a popular devotional figure known as Santo Niño de Atocha, or the Christ-child of Atocha. He is always portrayed wearing flowing robes and sandals. "This Niño travels around the world helping people and making miracles," my mother explained. Wherever they find his image, people leave sandals as an offering in the belief that he needs the footwear so he can walk about and tend to the devoted. My mom got me a Niño de Atocha candle. She told me to light it and say a prayer. We bought a pair of black baby Nike sandals and put them beneath the candle, and we

61

asked the Niño to be with my football team through the season.

It became a ritual for me to light the candle and pray after school on Fridays before I had to report to the football facility. My belief in the Niño took root and sprouted as Hope High School continued to win, plowing over teams on our journey toward the state championship. The buzz around school intensified as the season wore on and our prospects got better and better. We idolized the University of Arkansas Razorbacks, so we were elated when our team reached the state finals, which meant we would be playing on their home field—War Memorial Stadium in Little Rock, more than one hundred miles north of Hope.

Before the big game, my teammates and I did a walk-through at the Little Rock stadium, which seats more than fifty thousand fans. Butterflies whirled in my stomach. Emotions—pride, exhilaration, apprehension—burned through me as we filed in. I'd never set foot in such an enormous facility, and it was mind-blowing to think of all the amazing players who'd stepped on the same turf—the Razorbacks have contributed more than 250 players to the NFL over the years—not to mention the music legends, such as Elton John, George Strait, the Eagles, and the Rolling Stones, who had performed there.

In the locker room our team laced up cleats, lashed on pads, and made sure we were focused on the task at hand. The anticipation was sky-high as we trotted onto the field. I stood behind the banner the cheerleaders had prepared; it was probably the only time in my life I didn't care about the girls and wanted them to move out of the way.

Our opponents were from Greenville. On one punt return our guy was running with the ball and I saw someone about to tackle him. I ran toward the defender and put my best hit on this kid, completely blindsiding him so my teammate could gain a few more yards. I jumped around as if I had just won the game for us.

Unfortunately, we didn't have very many of those moments. The game got away from us, and our opponents began to feel the weight of the trophy in their hands. It was heartbreaking to look up at the scoreboard and see the lopsided numbers as the final seconds ticked down.

It was brutal having to walk over to the other side of the stadium to congratulate the winners. I stayed on the field and watched them celebrate before finally returning to the locker room to change. With a couple of teammates, I decided to go over to our opponents' locker room and offer our compliments.

"You were the better team," I said.

They applauded us for our efforts and thanked

us for being gracious. Somehow, that gesture made our loss less painful.

Still, we drove back to Hope with our heads down. Some players cried. Some just stared at the country road unraveling like a spool of ribbon toward home. The season was over.

And for me, so was Hope.

CHAPTER FIVE

Running Out of Hope

My mom had been seeing a man named Celestino for a while. Finally, she had landed a good guy, although he was very, very young—there was a twenty-three-year age difference between the two of them. My mom first met him one day when she was sitting in the break room at work, and the attraction was instantaneous—but she thought, *Oh, no.* He was closer to my age than to hers. All the African-American women at work teased her, calling her Stella, from *How Stella Got Her Groove Back*, the popular film based on the semiautobiographical Terry McMillan novel in which an older woman falls for a younger man.

Like Stella, my mom decided to take a chance, and Celestino became a mainstay in our lives. I was in early high school. Cele was a caring, calm man who absolutely cherished my mom. He thought of her as a little girl who needed to be taken care of. He always put her first, whether he was doing favors for her like cleaning up the house before she got home from work, or giving her little presents. He once brought her an artificial flower with a little doll inside because it reminded him of her.

It took me a while to warm up to him. I was still very leery of my mother's suitors after Hector. It was also a little embarrassing to deal with the remarks and questions I got from my friends about Cele's age. But once he won me over, the issues melted away. I never really looked at him like a father, though; he was more like a brother, but that worked fine. We had a lot of common interests, like basketball and video games, so when the weather was good we often went to the park to shoot hoops, and when it wasn't we'd stay inside and play NFL games on the Xbox.

On Memorial Day weekend 2001 the three of us decided to take a road trip to visit my mom's good friend Irma, who had moved to Dalton, Georgia, from Hope a few years earlier. My mom was godmother, or *madrina*, to Irma's daughter Carmen. My mom and I didn't get the chance to travel much, so we were looking forward to the trip. We planned to leave on Friday evening. It was a long drive, about six hundred miles due east across Arkansas through Tennessee, to Irma's small town in northeast Georgia. The drive would take us about ten hours, so we planned to travel through the night.

On Friday afternoon I left a football meeting at school and headed home, itching with excitement. My mom had our red Mitsubishi Galant packed and ready to go. Celestino settled into the backseat. My mom got into the front passenger seat, and I hopped behind the wheel.

I hadn't gotten around to taking the driving test for a license so was still driving with a learner's permit, but I prided myself on being an excellent driver. But as I steered the Mitsubishi slowly out of the apartment complex, my mom stopped me.

"Put on your seat belt, Rene," she ordered.

As an invincible teenager, about to turn seventeen, I viewed seat belts as an unnecessary restriction. I never wore one. But this day I didn't argue with my mom and buckled up—anything to get on our way.

We said a quick prayer for the Lord to keep us safe and get us to Georgia in one piece. I made a left turn onto the main road and was almost immediately greeted by flashing red, white, and blue lights. Ahead was a roadblock, a checkpoint for police to check cars for alcohol and drunk drivers.

I hadn't been drinking, and we were in a hurry, so over my mother's objections I made a quick U-turn to avoid the checkpoint.

"They're going to chase you!" my mom yelled.

I knew better. "No, Mom, it's fine. They won't even see me!"

But lights and sirens signaled that my mom was right. (Again.)

I pulled over into the only place I could, which

happened to be right back into the driveway of our apartment building. The officer approached my window. "Why did you turn around before the checkpoint?" he asked.

"We're on our way to Georgia. We've got a tight schedule," I answered. "I thought the checkpoint would slow us down." I'm sure that impressed him.

The officer asked for my driver's license. Since I only had a permit, I told him that my mom, a licensed driver, was in the car. The officer took my information and I relaxed, telling myself we'd be on the road again soon. The officer checked my mother's license, but that only made things worse: She still had her Louisiana license, even though we'd lived in Arkansas for something like nine years now. (She was a bit nostalgic; it was her first license and she wanted to keep it.)

Then the officer told me to step out. I did as I was told and walked to the rear of the car as he indicated. He handcuffed me and explained why I was being arrested. An outstanding warrant, he said. I felt light-headed as all the blood rushed out of my face. I could not believe this was happening.

The previous spring, my mom had wanted to go to the casino in Shreveport, about a two-hour drive from Hope. We occasionally made the trip so my mom could scratch her itch for the slots. Frequently she was pretty lucky—on some nights she could pull in about a thousand dollars, which was a lot of money for us. While she did her thing in the casino I'd spend that time waiting for her in the car, listening to music, napping, playing on my Game Boy. Sometimes I wandered into the lobby to buy a soda and people-watch. The groups of cute older girls particularly got my attention.

On this trip I was driving the three of us back home to Hope, my mom resting in the backseat after a long night of gambling, Cele dozing in the front. As the miles spiraled past on the lonely, rural two-lane road, my mom asleep, I started to wonder, *How fast can I get this Mitsubishi to go?* What can I say, I was sixteen. About twenty minutes from home, I got pulled over. I didn't have my permit yet, so my mom had to drive the rest of the way back, and I got a big, fat ticket.

A few months later, my mom, Celestino, and I were planning to bring in the new year at church. We'd bought a bunch of fireworks but had forgotten to take them with us for the celebration. My mom asked me and Celestino to go back to the apartment to get them.

On the way back to the church, I came up with a brilliant idea: "Wouldn't it be funny to throw some fireworks out the window?"

Don't ask me why, but we did it, tossing out a couple of Black Cats. Over our laughter, I heard sirens and saw lights behind me. When the officer asked me why I'd done it, I said, "Being stupid and not thinking at all." At least

69

I got that part right. I also got another ticket.

After the new year I called the courthouse to confirm the amount I owed on the tickets. The lady on the phone told me she only saw one ticket—the speeding citation—which I promptly paid. But that unpaid fireworks ticket had apparently morphed into a warrant.

And now the officer was telling me, "You're under arrest."

As soon as my mom saw the officer cuffing me, she jumped out of the car and began badgering him. "Why are you taking my son? What did he do?"

"Ma'am, please get back in the car."

Everybody knows you never get out of a car during a traffic stop unless a police officer tells you to. Everybody except my mom.

"You're supposed to be catching the gangsters and drug dealers, not a boy like him!" she yelled.

"Ma'am, get back in your car, or I'll take you, too," he warned. Even that didn't quiet her down. The officer looked over her head at me. "Son, tell your mother to simmer down or she's going to make this situation worse," he said.

She finally backed off, and I was helped into the backseat of the cruiser.

I tried to explain the ticket situation to the officer, and I apologized for my mom's behavior. Once we arrived at the station, he removed my handcuffs. After I waited for him to check my explanation of the tickets, he finally returned and handed me over to my mom.

And we were off again. Despite the delay, we made it to Dalton around nine o'clock on Saturday morning.

Dalton springs up from the foothills of the Blue Ridge Mountains. Home to about thirty thousand people, it has two claims to fame: It's the hometown of TV broadcaster Deborah Norville and the Carpet Capital of the World. But I didn't care about home furnishings and I didn't know who Deborah Norville was. What I liked was the town's vitality, something I believed was lacking back in Hope. I also noticed it had a sizable Hispanic community.

That afternoon, Irma and her family took us for a drive to Fort Mountain State Park. This is the southernmost portion of the Blue Ridge range, which extends northeast all the way to Pennsylvania. The highest peaks are in North Carolina and Tennessee, but the vistas in this part are still breathtaking.

As the weekend progressed, I couldn't shake the feeling that this was where I was meant to be.

"Hey, Mom, what do you think of this place?"

She was taken with it as well.

The next day, our last of the visit, was spent driving around Dalton looking at the stores and businesses. We took another trip into the mountains, where we swam in a lake, still ice-cold from the spring runoff. My mom and Irma watched from a nearby picnic table, talking.

The next morning we hit the road back to Hope—but I was already plotting a move. I had been frustrated by the shortage of opportunity in Hope. The lukewarm ambition among my class-mates and the scarcity of people like me—other than my friend Juan—frequently made me feel like an outsider there. And once I had my sights set on football, I understood that Hope wasn't the place for me. My goal of playing pro football was still ping-ponging around in my skull, and I'd always heard that the game was king in places such as Texas, Florida, and Georgia. *If I were there,* I thought, *maybe someone who could offer me a bigger opportunity would see me play.*

I've never been the most patient person, and now that I had Georgia in my sights, I wanted to get there as quickly as possible. I felt sure that if I didn't go after my dream right away, it would evaporate.

My mom was very reluctant to leave Hope, however. She had a great job at Tyson Foods, where she'd recently been promoted. She was making more money than everyone but her supervisors, had a 401(k) and paid vacation. This was a huge deal for a woman who'd bused tables for so long, and she was afraid to leave it. Would she be able to find another job like that in Dalton?

Irma was also encouraging us to move, and she assured my mom it was a smart thing to do. Mom finally relented.

I was ecstatic about my mom's change of heart. I thought this was going to be a great new beginning for both of us.

After she went to bed that night, I yanked all our pictures off the wall and piled them up and found a few boxes for our things.

"What did you do?" she yelled the next morning.

"You said we were moving," I answered, "so I started packing."

She rolled her eyes. "We can't go right now! We have to pay our bills and save our money."

Later that week, Irma called again to check on our progress. The economy was in a downturn, she told us, and job opportunities in Georgia were starting to decline, too. If we delayed any longer, we could find ourselves in a tight spot.

I decided it made sense to move right away. Celestino was keen to see what opportunities were out there, too. So he and I hatched a plan to go for a few weeks over the summer and look around, try to find work. If it didn't happen, we'd return to Hope and that would be that.

On June 14, 2001, we celebrated my eighteenth birthday. My cake was topped by my baby picture and eighteen candles. But the gift was what I really prized—a seventy-five-dollar one-way Greyhound ticket out of Hope.

73

On Saturday, June 16, Celestino and I boarded the bus for the fifteen-hour ride back to Georgia. It stopped in Memphis at dinnertime and I called my mom to let her know we were okay. We rode on through the night, the bus making stops in towns along the way.

We rattled over the Georgia line and into a town called Dalton, but it was dark, the place was deserted, and we were tired, so it didn't register that we were in *the* Dalton, which is how we found ourselves in the Atlanta bus terminal several hours later. The next bus back to Dalton wasn't until morning. We spent a long night in the station, alternately trying to sleep and playing pinball, making sure we didn't miss our bus. The people-watching was fantastic. I was fascinated to see people from different walks of life— homeless, elderly—who wandered the halls. *Who is that man?* I'd think. *Where's he going and what's his story?* I wondered if I'd look like them in twenty or a hundred years.

At ten the next morning we made it to Dalton, greeted by handshakes at the bus terminal by Irma's husband, Javier.

Monday morning, we hit the ground running. "I'm getting a job today," I told Celestino. I was beyond determined and would pound the pavement until someone hired me.

Irma let us borrow their minivan. Our first stop was Shaw Industries, a furnishings, flooring, and carpet manufacturer. I had no idea what I was getting myself into. My only previous job experience was working as a dishwasher at Little B's Mexican and Steak House in Hope. It took some time to fill out the applications because I had to do Celestino's as well as my own, since his English was limited. I did the best I could, trying to accurately represent his work experience back at the poultry plant in Hope. I had to guess at his education level, because the system in Mexico is so different from ours.

When I finished and handed the documents to the receptionist, she asked us what positions we were looking for.

"Anything you have," I said, hoping my smile would make a difference.

She told us to take a seat and wait; someone would look over our applications and see us soon. We waited, and waited, and waited. After lunch we were called into individual interviews with a couple of Shaw reps. Mine was from Guatemala. I think his name was Rene, too.

"I only have experience in a restaurant, but I'm willing to learn any position because I want to move here," I told him. I really had no clue. I just knew I had to get a job for this move to happen.

That evening we called my mom to tell her the big news: We had jobs!

The next day, Tuesday, Celestino and I attended

orientation at Shaw, where we were briefed about our jobs, the safety rules, the pay scales, and the history of the company. I learned I would be a forklift driver for a shipping and receiving plant. I'd never driven a forklift in my life, but that didn't bother me. I only cared that I had a job, and this job was going to pay me $250 a week— good money for an eighteen-year-old.

That night I reported to work for the 11 p.m. to 8 a.m. shift, graveyard. My job consisted of unloading rolls of carpet off the eighteen-wheelers and storing them in the warehouses. I was a little nervous because the other men there seemed to be old hands; they looked at me like, "Who the hell is the new kid?"

I wasn't very good at the job. It was nerve-racking work and I was afraid to mess up and lose this precious opportunity, but I found a way to make it through my shift every night. It was exhausting. I'd punch out in the morning, pick up Celestino at his workplace down the road, and be showered and in bed by 9 a.m. There wasn't a whole lot to life.

One night I was talking to another worker about playing football in Dalton. "Do you know which schools have the best football programs?" I asked him. He told me Dalton High School had a forty-plus-year streak of winning seasons. Good to know.

But before I could even think about football

season and my senior year, I had a more pressing goal: saving enough money for a place to live. My mom arrived in Dalton on July 4 driving a U-Haul truck packed with our belongings, a trailer with her car riding on it following right behind her. She squeezed in with us into Irma's crowded little house.

The Monday after she got to town, my mother went to Shaw to apply for a job. She wasn't as lucky as we had been. "We'll call you," they told her, and sent her on her way. Celestino and I carried on at our shifts and saved our money. We continued to live off the generosity of Irma.

But when my mom got the callback offering a job in the factory a few weeks later, we celebrated with a Mexican dinner out.

Hoarding my paychecks, I first paid the $400 for the outstanding ticket in Hope. By August 1, we had all managed to save enough for the $700 deposit on a two-bedroom apartment and the $175 weekly rent we'd spend to live there.

Now it was time to focus on school and I was eager because the start of football practice was just a few weeks away. We visited Dalton High, home of the Catamounts. The football program reliably sent a handful of guys to college every year on athletic scholarships. Nine guys had gone to football powerhouses like the University of Georgia and Auburn the previous year alone.

In a town like Dalton, high school sports brings the community together, and football is huge. Football means a sense of honor, pride, and tradition. Buzz Bissinger's bestselling book *Friday Night Lights*, an account of a school in Dillon, Texas (a successful television series followed), could have described Dalton, too. If there was a Friday night game, you could be sure the stadium would be packed with five thousand or more spectators, some sitting in seats that had been bought and paid for by local families for years.

Dalton High was about 60 percent Hispanic, 30 percent white, and 10 percent African-American or other race. I loved the fact that there would be so many students who looked like me.

"I like this place already," I told my mom, checking out the huge catamount (mountain lion) mural sweeping across one wall. I felt a good energy in the place and could imagine myself hanging out there.

While my mom worked out the details of my transfer, I asked the principal for the phone number of the football coach, Ronnie McClurg. When we got home, I called him. As soon as he answered, I didn't miss a beat. "Hi, Coach, my name is Jose Martinez. I just moved here from Arkansas for my senior year and I want to play for your team."

His response punched me in the gut.

"We don't take seniors unless you're a starter or a first-team substitute," he replied.

I was devastated, but I held it in. "I understand your policy," I said, "but all I'm asking for is an opportunity to try out for the team."

There was a pause as I waited anxiously, hearing only my racing heart. This man had my future in his hands.

"Okay," he said. "You can come out and we'll see if there's a slot for you."

I was too new to Dalton to know this at the time, but Coach McClurg was a venerated figure in the community. Now seventy-one, he was an educator for forty years—starting as a science teacher, moving into the physical education department, and spending the last decade of his career as Dalton High's athletic director and head football coach.

So if Coach McClurg said no, it was going to be no. Even so, I hung up feeling confident. While I'd never been the most talented on the football field, I had a tremendous amount of self-assurance and a strong work ethic. Even though size and speed weren't in my favor, I had never let myself be pushed around by the bigger or faster players. I played harder than my size warranted. I was full of heart and the will to fight for my goal of making it to the top. I knew that my ankle injury wouldn't allow me to play 100 percent—I was still hobbling from the surgery

I'd had the previous spring—but I also believed I could compensate with guts and the sheer force of my personality.

The first day of tryouts before the school year officially began was pretty awkward as I walked onto the field not knowing a soul, the other guys all staring at the new kid.

Coach McClurg pulled me aside and grilled me: Where are you from? Why do you want to play football?

My answers were straightforward: "I'm from Louisiana and Arkansas. Football is my dream and I love the game."

Coach lined us up on the field. I noticed during the drills that when some guys messed up and made a bad play, they'd walk off the field with their heads down. I immediately went over to pat them on the back. While the others were on the field, I clapped and yelled out encouragement. I'm sure the guys were wondering who in the world I was, yelling like that, but it felt so good to be part of a team again.

After the tryouts Coach McClurg called me into his office. Heart pounding, I sat down.

"I want you to know that you just made the team," he said. "It has nothing to do with your ability and everything to do with your attitude." That was a magic moment.

I'd already learned back in Hope that football was key to my acceptance among the other students. Starting at a new school for my senior year would be especially challenging, coming in when the other kids had been forming bonds for years. I knew that being on the team would ease the transition. I decided something else right then: No more Jose for me. I didn't want to use my father's name—Jose—and Rene didn't appeal to me. I was tired of going by that name and wanted to create my own identity. I told Coach McClurg to call me J.R. It was a new beginning, so why not go all the way?

And sure enough, when the double doors to Dalton High swung open in September, I made friends, both male and female, quickly. Soon, girls would sit next to me in class or during lunch and play with my hair, twirling it around their fingers. Some guys were annoyed that I was getting so much attention, and I really didn't blame them. My well-considered response was always the same: "I'm the new guy—that's the only reason they like me."

Tracy Gonzalez was my best girlfriend—friend who was a girl, I mean. We had a math class together and clicked right off the bat, like brother and sister. After games, we'd hang out at a place called Steak n' Shake and annoy the waitstaff.

Tracy complained that girls were always trying to befriend her to get to me. They'd ask her, "What are you and J.R. doing this weekend?" They interrogated her about which girls I was talking to, whether I liked anyone. She called me "the honey to the bees."

I certainly enjoyed basking in the attention of Dalton High's women, but that fall I focused like a laser on football. Just football. I played outside linebacker on defense and I was on special teams. I was a role player and a motivator and helped the guys get better in practice by encouraging them and working hard myself.

Every Thursday night after practice, all the team's seniors would gather at the clubhouse in a beautiful gated community for what was called Senior Night. Many of the senior players' moms would be there, and they'd cook us dinners of spaghetti or fried chicken. The players would gather downstairs where there was a pool table, couches, and TV. As the team leaders, we'd talk about the next night's game.

But early in the season, we received a huge jolt. I had my head down on my desk, as I often did during the first periods of the morning—my bad habits in the classroom had followed me from Hope—when a friend tapped me on the shoulder to rouse me. I lifted my head and there, on the television, I saw airplanes hitting tall buildings in New York City, flames erupting, firefighters lumbering in, and people running out. At that moment I couldn't know how profoundly that event would change my life.

After the initial shock of those images, I went back to being a typical teenager with visions of football stardom and girls.

Our football team was having another fantastic season. We had a strong lineup, and there were early murmurings that we could make it to the state championship once again.

Antoine Simmons, one of Dalton High's athletic trainers, used to practice his Spanish on me. Before a game, he'd always ask me if I was ready. "*Listo*?" he'd say.

One night he asked me the usual question, and for some reason I answered, "*Listo para guerra.*" I'm ready for war.

Our team enjoyed huge success. We made it to the state championship, although we didn't win. But another five Catamount guys would go on to college on football scholarships that year.

My first real girlfriend in Dalton was Daniela, a fifteen-year-old freshman. She rolled with the rich white girls and had a preppy air about her, but her family was Colombian and, like me, she was being raised by a single mom. It was no secret that I was a big flirt, but for some reason until Daniela I hadn't committed to a relationship with anyone. That said, Daniela was sweet and definitely cute, but I never felt like I was in love with her, and I was careful never to tell her any different. Nonetheless, one night we talked about sex and she surprised me by volunteering that she was ready for it. She wasn't my first, but I was hers. Since she'd never done it before, I tried not to be an ass, taking great care to make her comfortable in her nervousness. After that first time, we weren't able to be alone too often, but when we were, we'd take advantage of the situation, if you know what I mean.

In the early spring, I informed my mom that I wanted to go to college, too. Since I wanted to be a pro player, I needed to play the game at the university level. I didn't care about the academics —I just cared about football. My mom, on the other hand, wanted me to go to college so that I could get a job in Dalton as a doctor, a lawyer, an architect. She wanted to see me wear a suit.

A teammate of mine named Aaron Ward had a brother who was thinking of attending the University of West Georgia in Carrollton, about a two-hour drive from Dalton. The Ward brothers' father, Ron, was the assistant principal at our school. Their stepmom, Susan, was a middle school English teacher. They'd always welcomed me into their home, and now they invited me and my mom to join them on a campus tour of UWG.

As we walked the campus, I pictured myself playing football as a UWG Brave (this was before they changed their names to the Wolves because of controversy over the use of a Native American term). The team was part of the Gulf South Conference of NCAA Division II.

At the tail end of the tour. I got the chance to speak to a counselor about my potential admission. He looked at my records and then fixed his gaze squarely at me. "Sorry, son," he said. "You're not eligible to play football at the college level." I didn't have enough credits at that moment. It hadn't occurred to me that I might be turned away, and I was crushed. Now what?

At the beginning of my senior year, my Dalton High counselor had told me that I needed more credits toward graduation than I'd be able to earn in a regular school year. I was shocked and ashamed, though I knew very well there was no one to blame but myself. The fact is, I was more dedicated to being everything except a good student. I chose that road because I didn't understand the advantage of good grades nor did I know how school could help me in the long run. Also, I hadn't really noted the fact that I needed to complete certain specific classes for graduation.

Since college football now seemed out of the question, the effort of making up the credits would be for my mother. I didn't want her to feel as if I had been half-assed about my schoolwork (although I had) when she had worked so hard to give me everything. I begged the counselor for options. Again, I thought about my mother and what a privilege it would have been for her to get an education past the third grade. I felt ashamed of once again not focusing and taking my opportunities for granted. How many second chances would I get in life?

The counselor had recommended night school, but I had to wait until the spring because my fall semester was dominated by football. Monday through Thursday nights, from six to ten o'clock, I dragged through two classes from dinner until bedtime. Usually I'd go straight from school to Sonic, the burger chain where I worked a shift, and then on to night school. It was anything but fun, but I felt that I could and would do anything to be able to graduate with the rest of my classmates.

I busted my ass in night school and was rewarded when my mom got to see me walk across the stage with my Dalton High classmates to receive my diploma. But that thrill faded as quickly as the applause. I had nowhere to go and not a lot to do. I managed to get an inventory job at a local cable company, and all day long I'd count splitters, cable lines, and screws. I found the job incredibly boring and I hated it.

During my off hours I lay around, dejected and moping, watching hours of sports on ESPN. I berated myself for believing I could go to college and make something of myself. I began to panic about what I would do for the rest of my life. Work at a monotonous job for the next fifty years? Again and again I asked myself: *What are you going to do with your life?* I hadn't considered a single option. I guessed I really was a Multi-cultural Idiot.

Until the day a commercial for the U.S. Army came on. Be all that you can be. It spoke right to me.

CHAPTER SIX

Uncle Sam Wants Me

"I'm going to enlist."

"Mijo, what?"

Military recruiters had come to Dalton High a few months before graduation. At the time, I had convinced myself I was going to go to college to play football so I only half-listened to the recruiters' pitch.

But now their words came back to me—opportunity, patriotism, a chance to see the world. I could save money for college in case I eventually decided to enroll. I would be more independent and it would allow me to give back to the country that had given so much to my mother and me.

My mom wasn't so thrilled. Having experienced the horrors of Salvadoran civil war firsthand, she had a very real fear of losing me. And I knew she thought often of my sister Anabel, the child she'd already lost, not to mention her other daughter left behind in El Salvador. She was fully aware that the war in Afghanistan had begun on October 7, 2001, less than a month after the planes hit the

Twin Towers in New York, the Pentagon in Arlington, Virginia, and crashed near Shanksville, Pennsylvania. And while Operation Iraqi Freedom technically would not launch until March 19, 2003, U.S. troops had been gearing up for months in preparation for the invasion.

On September 11, 2002, my mother drove me to Walnut Square Mall to meet with the recruiter before I'd board a van for an overnight trip to the Armed Forces Recruiting Center in Knoxville, Tennessee. Once there, I would be required to pass several tests to clear the way for enlistment. (I'd already made the trip to Fort Knox a few times during the summer for initial tests.) Assuming all went well, from there I'd go straight to Basic Combat Training at Fort Benning, Georgia, home to the U.S. Army Infantry School.

At his office, the recruiter handed me some documents to fill out. While she waited, my mom looked around the office. She concentrated on framed photos of kids who had recently enlisted and others of those who'd already been in the Army for some time. Some showed soldiers in the field, and I could see those made her sad. At the same time, she was proud to know that I was willing to step up and wear the uniform, that I would be a man.

But when I was finished with the forms, she reminded me that I was still her little boy. "Mijo, you have to eat," she said.

I looked at the recruiter. "Do I have time to grab something before we leave?"

He nodded. "It will be a little while before the van arrives for you."

We found a Chinese place and sat down to have one last meal together. My friend Gabriel joined us. We talked and joked about everything except the fact that I was leaving. We walked back through the mall to the recruiter's office, laughing.

The van arrived and the driver appeared in the office. "Where's the young man I'll be taking?" he asked.

I stood up and reality sank in. At the van the driver grabbed my bag and threw it into the rear of the vehicle. I put my arms around my mother. Though I felt enthusiastic about this step, I was suddenly frightened of the unknown. I was going to be away for a long time.

I took one last look at my mother, who gave me a wide smile that couldn't hide the fear in her eyes.

I settled in for the two-hour ride to Knoxville.

When we arrived, I checked into my hotel room and headed down to the recreational area reserved for those of us who planned to swear in the following morning. It had been a long day, but I was restless. I decided to take a walk into town to see the sights.

My goal was to check out the stadium where the University of Tennessee Volunteers played. I wasn't a fan of the team, but Celestino was, and I figured it would be cool to see it. I wandered the streets and sidewalks, feeling foolish and wondering why I hadn't thought to consult a map or ask someone for guidance. I finally stumbled on the campus and made my way to Neyland Stadium, which accommodates more than one hundred thousand fans.

I stopped at a pay phone to call my mom and Celestino to describe it. It was fun to hear Cele's excitement but it was bittersweet for me, because I saw my college dreams on that bright green field. I imagined the spectators filling those seats to cheer for me and my teammates.

As I began the long walk back to my hotel, I changed my focus from the regrets of the past to the future. Tomorrow I would become a soldier.

The *brrrrinngggg* of the phone broke the dark quiet of my room at 3 a.m. with a wake-up call. Back in Dalton, my mother also woke early. She put on her makeup, an ocean-blue blouse, and heels. She, Celestino, Daniela, and Gabriel met to begin the two-hour drive from Dalton to Knoxville to see me sworn in to the U.S. Army.

When they arrived, I pulled my mother into a big bear hug before acknowledging anyone else. We walked into the building where the ceremony would be conducted and sat down to wait. Eight other young men were there for the same reason. An officer entered the room. We lined up and one by one recited the Armed Forces Oath of Enlistment:

I, Jose Rene Martinez, do solemnly swear that I will support and defend the Constitution of the United States against all enemies, foreign and domestic; that I will bear true faith and allegiance to the same; and that I will obey the orders of the President of the United States and the orders of the officers appointed over me, according to regulations and the Uniform Code of Military Justice. So help me God.

I was officially the property of the U.S. Army, a soldier. I felt an unanticipated, physical surge of pride as the officer shook my hand, his eyes meeting mine.

My mom's disposable camera clicked and whirred. The snapshots from that day show me in a white T-shirt, black jeans, and the new Nikes I'd bought to train for the Army physical fitness test. My hair is cut short on the sides and curly on the top, and I have a skinny mustache.

Everyone hugged me one last time, and my mother cried.

"I love you, mijo," she whispered, her arms tight around my waist. "I'm proud of you. Be strong. And you'd better write to me."

I boarded the van and found a seat alone for the five-hour ride to Fort Benning. My mom wanted to follow the van as far as she could. I looked out the window and watched my gold 1996 Nissan Maxima trailing with my loved ones inside. That made me smile. After a while they fell back.

I slipped in the earbuds to my CD player, trying to calm myself with some music. Nelly and Tim McGraw's "Over and Over" came on, and I started to cry soundless tears.

Despite the burgeoning homesickness, I was excited about this adventure. I wasn't thinking about the drill sergeants who would be yelling in my face. I actually thought of it like going away to football camp. I was looking forward to living somewhere else with new people, hanging around a bunch of dudes, pushing each other and sharing laughs. Boy, was I in for a rude awakening.

I arrived at Fort Benning on the evening of September 12. I was pleased to find that everyone was pretty nice, and I started to think that it was going to be exactly as I had imagined.

The next morning we were herded into the barbershop, and that hair the girls had long admired ended up in a pile to be swept off the floor. For the first time I could remember, I felt a breeze on my scalp.

One by one we privates stood for our basic training photos. The drill sergeants told us to look mean because we were infantrymen, tough and unfriendly. My turn came and without thinking I broke into a giant smile, corner to corner. This earned me a lot of teasing.

From there we boarded buses to go to our unit areas. We were ordered to sit with our heads down so that we wouldn't be able to see where we were going. I tried several times to sneak a peek but the sergeant caught me. After a while, the bus crawled to a stop.

I heard men yelling outside. "Get off the bus!"

I'd just had a quiet ride resting my head, and now this? The second I stepped down there was a man in my face.

"Get down! Get down! Give me push-ups!"

It was almost funny when I heard one of the drill sergeants say to no one in particular, but loud enough to mock us, "Dear Mom, I've made a mistake!"

Once the drill sergeants made their unpleasant introductions, they rushed us into the barracks that would be our home for the next few months.

"Drop your gear and hit the floor!"

I'd thought the push-ups phase was over. But no. In the Army it's called "smoking." It's a form of hazing, or a "corrective measure," whereby privates are compelled to repeat an exercise, such as push-ups, until the bosses decide they can stop. I probably did a few hundred push-ups that first day, until my arms were quivering and numb.

The drill sergeants assigned each recruit a "battle buddy," or partner. With the battle-buddy system, each soldier is paired with another guy and expected to keep an eye on each other to improve safety and protection during battle. In boot camp, you're ordered to stay near your battle buddy—always. Mine was a tall African-American guy, a few years older than me, from New York City. He didn't say much, but he had a lot of swagger.

We took our first trip to the chow hall—walking in a straight line, eyes fixed on the shaved heads in front of us—and wolfed down our food. Back in line, I realized that my battle buddy wasn't next to me. I panicked. I could guess what would happen to me when the drill sergeants noticed. Without thinking, I made eye contact with one of the drill instructors. Big mistake.

He strutted over to me, frowning. "Why are you looking at me, boy? You like me or something?"

"No."

"No what?" he fired back.

"No, I don't like you."

"That's wrong!" he yelled. "From now on you will say, 'No, Drill Sergeant.' "

Then the DI noticed the space next to me that my battle buddy didn't occupy.

"Where is your battle buddy?" he demanded, his eyes boring into me.

I gulped. "I don't know, Drill Sergeant."

He pulled me out of the line. "I'm going to smoke you till your battle buddy shows up!" he yelled. "Even if it makes you throw up the food you just ate!"

I flashed on something my recruiter had told me before I left for basic: "Make sure the drill sergeants don't know your name. If they find out, you're in trouble."

"What's your name, Private?" the drill sergeant demanded.

I was gasping for air as I heaved myself down and up, down and up in push-ups. "Martinez!" I huffed. So here I'd been at basic for only a few hours, and I was already screwed. It was officially over. He knew my name.

"Well, Martinez," he said, "if your battle buddy doesn't show up soon, then you and I have reservations for a date later." I knew this wasn't a date I wanted.

For the next half hour, that date was all I thought about. My battle buddy finally showed up.

"Where the hell have you been?" I asked him.

"I got lost leaving the chow hall," he said.

"We were all in a single-file line," I said. "All you had to do was follow everyone else!"

He frowned at me. Clearly he didn't care that because of him I'd already been personally introduced to the drill sergeants.

As my group unpacked our few belongings and loaded them into our lockers, the drill sergeants leaned over us, checking every tiny detail, smoking us when things didn't look right. The folding techniques I learned in basic follow me to this day. I can fit almost anything into a small bag, just like in a game of Tetris.

Next, we were invited to shower, basic-style. It had been such a hard day already and I looked forward to a nice, long, hot shower—a little water massage on my tired muscles, some time to relax. My mind drifted into fantasy, but the drill sergeants brought me back to reality real quick. We were instructed to grab our Dopp kits—that's a man purse for grooming items, for all you ladies and civilians—run to the community showers, and report back within a couple of *minutes.* I barely had time to wash my newly shaved skull. At least I got a good laugh watching everyone slipping and sliding as they ran in and out of the showers. One guy hadn't even washed the soap from his head.

The first day of basic wound down. I couldn't wait to climb into my bed to catch some z's. But we were informed that we would be woken up at 4 a.m. I already missed those days when I could sleep in. But for now, this was my life. I peeled back the green Army-issue blanket and starched white sheet and crawled in, laying my prickly head on the flat slab that was supposed to be a pillow. I thought this wasn't going to be nearly as enjoyable as I'd assumed it would be, and then I fell into an exhausted sleep.

Maybe ten minutes passed before the world exploded. The drill sergeants rushed into the bay, yelling and banging things. Recruits were a tangle of arms and legs, all struggling to respond to the chaos.

"Get downstairs and line up!" the DIs screamed.

A couple of guys didn't make it down the stairs before the DIs, so the entire group paid the price and we all got smoked. From sound asleep to push-ups within thirty seconds.

Since I was an athlete, I was in good shape. But the lack of food, sleep, and peace made me wonder if I would last. When the sun finally rose, the DIs sent us inside to get dressed, with orders to hurry up and come back for breakfast. Breakfast was drunk, not chewed—no time for chewing.

Two weeks went by at about the same pace. It seemed like the drill sergeants all hated life, and they were taking it out on us. Then, imperceptibly, it began to change. The DIs somehow became a little less mean. The mornings became more of a challenge than a calamitous rush.

By then I had a few friends: Alex from Fresno, Matthew from Wisconsin, and PJ from Nebraska. Everyone called PJ "Nebraska" and everyone called me "Georgia." Our last names were close together alphabetically, so we bunked side by side.

Pretty much right away PJ had stood out—he had a mouth on him. I stood out, too, for the same reason. In fact, PJ later told me that the DIs had told him not to hang out with me, a warning he disregarded. It wasn't so much that I challenged authority, although sometimes I did; the real problem was that I would make everyone laugh when I did smart-alecky things. There was a guy from Minnesota who had the thickest Midwestern accent I'd ever heard. I couldn't stop myself from imitating him, which never failed to get snickers from the entire company. PJ craved attention like me. That was another trait that drew us together.

While other recruits in basic talk about pretty girls and fast cars, I'd talk about my mom a lot. People would make those "your mama" jokes, and I wouldn't go along. I made it clear to others that it was off-limits to talk about my mom. The truth was, I missed her a lot.

I couldn't even imagine how much she missed me. It was many long days before we were allowed to make our first phone call home. Even then, that call lasted just thirty seconds, long enough for me to say, "I'm here, I love you, goodbye." A few days later we got a little more phone time and I was able to chat with her a bit longer, assuring her that I was okay and giving her a blow-by-blow of the routine.

Beyond that, opportunities for phone calls didn't come very often. Instead, we wrote letters—carefully printed on ripped-out notebook paper. I'd never written so much in my life. Who could've guessed that I'd do more writing in basic than I had during four years of high school? Many of my letters were addressed to Daniela. She wrote back, sometimes sealing the envelope with a lipstick imprint. I told her I missed her, but I felt us growing apart. Here I was training to be a soldier, and she still had three more years of high school.

I quickly grew impatient waiting for the next time we were authorized to use the phone, so I came up with a better idea.

Once our schedules loosened up a bit, we had free time in the evening to write letters, do laundry, or just hang out. PJ, Alex, me, and a few of the others would use the time to jog around the barracks, reasoning that we were improving our endurance, thereby making basic easier. We just weren't allowed to stray beyond the perimeter of our barracks.

However, there were other barracks nearby. So one night, Matthew, Alex, and I decided to sneak over to use the phones there. The stakes were high, but eighteen-year-olds are notorious gamblers, although the three of us differed in how risk averse we were. Matthew was at one end—a big risk taker who didn't mind using his tough-guy attitude to get what he wanted. Alex's approach bordered on paranoid. I was in the middle: I didn't mind taking chances but I usually first gave them some consideration. But this plan looked simple to all of us.

We jogged around the building like always, but then instead of looping back, we continued right over to the other barracks. Since no recruits occupied the area by the phones, it wasn't lit. We were pinching ourselves: How much better could this have worked out? We were in a dark corner using the phones and no one in our company knew about it. We each had a leisurely ten-minute phone call with our loved ones, then headed back.

This was too easy for us not to try again . . . and again. One night, as we were yammering away on our calls, we saw a drill sergeant walking by, dangerously close. We stopped speaking into the phones and squatted. Alex became very nervous and was poised to run but we talked him into staying put. The drill sergeant walked on by, and our deception continued to work smoothly.

However, I've learned many things in life, and one of them is that when you break the rules, you will be caught.

A few nights later, we jogged away to do our thing, breaking off our route to head toward the phones. Once again a drill sergeant walked by. But this time Alex couldn't contain himself and headed for the hills. The sound of his footsteps alerted the drill sergeant.

"Hey, Private, stop!"

Matthew and I took off running. We cut through the vacant barracks and maneuvered our way around the building, so if the drill sergeant was on our tails he wouldn't see which barracks we entered. We got to ours, hearts pounding. Our fellow recruits looked on curiously.

But where was Alex? Then we heard a drill sergeant yelling outside in the main area. We peeked out the window to see Alex being chewed out and smoked by the drill sergeant. I wish I could say that Matthew and I jumped to Alex's defense. Instead, we snuck back to our bunks and tried to figure whether he would tell on us.

About thirty minutes passed before Alex showed up, red-faced and bathed in sweat.

"How did you get caught when you left before us?" we asked him.

After catching his breath, he told us that he ran into the laundry building and hid under the table.

We burst out laughing: Why on earth would you run into a room that was right around the corner when the drill sergeant could see you run into it? This explained why the drill sergeant hadn't followed me and Matthew.

Alex said he hadn't told on us. Relief washed over us.

"What did the drill sergeant do besides smoke you?" we asked.

"He said he would be telling our drill sergeants about it so they can do more with it."

That made us more than a little nervous. Our drill sergeants likely would figure out who the other two guys were.

Days passed before one of our drill sergeants, with all the recruits in formation, asked about the other two guys. Cowed, Matthew and I stood in silence. When no one spoke up, the drill sergeants dismissed us all with a parting thought: "We will find out, and when we do, you will be sorry."

Once the DIs departed, one of the other privates in our group said, "We know it was you. If you don't fess up, we'll do it for you."

But days turned into weeks, no one ratted, and the matter was never addressed again. Talk about dodging a bullet.

But I found other ways to irritate my classmates. One day during bad weather, we had to train inside using a shooting simulator. With just a couple of simulators and more than forty guys, the rotation was slow and there was a lot of time doing nothing. I got bored.

In between yawns, I came up with a plan to get a few more minutes of shut-eye. I told the others I was going to the restroom. Once there, I sat down on the toilet to make it seem as if I actually was using the facilities. I pulled down my shorts to my ankles to sell the point. I nodded out with my elbows digging into my thighs and cheeks resting on my hands, the most comfortable position I could maneuver myself into.

I was jolted awake by a yell. "Martinez!" The person sounded panicky. "Martinez!" yelled another.

"I'm here!"

A couple of privates ran up to the stall door. "Everyone's lined up outside in formation!"

"How long have I been in here?"

"At least an hour. We forgot all about you."

I knew I had about two seconds to get to formation before the drill sergeants noticed I was missing, and then all of us would pay for it. I tried to stand up. My legs buckled and I crumpled to the ground, my shorts around my knees.

"My legs are asleep!" I shouted. "I can't walk!" I managed to unlatch the door. The guys pushed it open and reached in to help me stand.

Then they took a good look at me. "Why are your shorts halfway down?"

Oh God. "To make it believable that I was using the restroom!"

They just shook their heads. I got the shorts up, put each arm over the guys, and hobbled out of the barracks until my legs began to work again. Once they were completely functional, I was able to do a full sprint to the formation and made it just in time.

On another occasion, our class went out for field-training exercises, or FTX, armed with our rucksacks, sleeping bags, and MREs, those self-contained rations. As a kid I'd listened to my friends talk about camping trips they'd taken with their families or the Boy Scouts. It had sounded like so much fun, but I'd never had the opportunity to experience it. So going into the field was exciting for me, because I felt like I was camping with friends. The purpose was to practice what we'd learned in the classroom: perform first aid on a manikin, react to contact, run through battle drills.

One training exercise was called a flanking maneuver, an attack around the side of an opposing force. This means we can hit the enemy from the side or the rear. These exercises were designed, of course, to ready us for combat. Someday we all could find ourselves within reach of the enemy. But for now, it was just plain fun, like playing paintball.

We privates had to sleep in a big circle, our locations dictated alphabetically by last name. I wasn't near my friend Alex, but I wanted to be. One night he pulled his sleeping bag over to my area so we could hang out. This particular night I was roused for my shift to pull security. The guy coming off handed me a watch so I could time my segment. We had just enough recruits in our platoon to require everyone to stand watch for an hour by morning.

I sat up in my warm sleeping bag and woke up Alex to pull the shift with me.

"I'm so tired," he moaned.

"Me, too," I said. "And it's freezing out here."

That's when another brilliant idea struck me. "Since we have to do two hours, go back to sleep," I told him. "I'll wake you at the one-hour mark to finish off the shift." Alex grunted his agreement and burrowed back down.

It was frigid and dark, and I was tired. All around me men were snoring and making other disgusting sounds as they slept fitfully on the hard ground. My eyes grew heavy and my head started to bob down. This just wasn't going to work for me.

Maybe ten minutes into my shift, I pushed the time forward by one hour and fifty minutes on the watch. I shook the next guy and told him it was his shift.

Alex woke up and asked, "When is it my turn?"

"No worries. I took care of it."

He rolled over and went back to sleep as I folded into my sleeping bag.

Hours later I woke up to the sound of trainees loudly arguing about someone having to pull a double shift. One guy said, "If everyone had done their one hour, no one would have had to do two shifts."

I stayed quiet until Alex approached me and asked me if I had anything to do with this, since he hadn't done his shift. I whispered, "Let's just say time flew when I was on duty." I smiled and kept on moving.

Everyone else continued to argue about the clock

and how someone had skipped out on his duty. All except me. I understood it had been a selfish move. Yeah, it sucked to see everybody at one another's throats, but I wasn't about to step up and confess, because they'd kick my ass.

I knew it was wrong, but I reasoned that it was only basic training. It wasn't like we were in combat. We were in the middle of the woods in Georgia. No one was going to get hurt. I figured I was just getting away with something. When I look back on this incident, I feel embarrassed but glad to know that I've come a long way since then.

Basic training showed me a lot about myself, both good and bad. I was able to prove to myself that I was strong, but I also knew that I still had a lot of growing up to do.

It also brought some fears to the surface. For example, our drill sergeants trained us to low-crawl up to a blank claymore mine and defuse its wires. I broke multiple sweats thinking about how I might be required to defuse a live mine. What if I accidentally triggered it? How would the impact feel? How would it damage my face and body? What if my mistake hurt someone else? What if I died?

One day, one of our drill instructors paced among us as we recruits sat on the floor and explained, "It's not *if* you'll deploy, it's *when*." Some of us glanced at each other, nervous but psyched.

He reminded us that the hard days and nights here in basic were preparation. "The way we break you down isn't for our own enjoyment," he said. "The training and skills we are drilling into you will help save your lives and those of your fellow soldiers someday."

I wondered if I'd really be sent to Iraq. But the concept was so abstract at the time, it didn't bother me much.

Thirteen weeks on, as I looked toward graduation, I had become a young man who could face the unknown, who could make new buddies out of a room of strangers, and who was able to push myself through challenges far more difficult than I'd imagined. I was proud of what I'd achieved.

In December 2002 I stood at attention in my green Class B short-sleeved uniform, eyes forward, spine straight, listening to one of our drill sergeants address the platoon.

My mom was in the spectator viewing area. She barely recognized me onstage.

After the Pass and Review (I was really good at marching, by the way) and the ceremony concluded, we were cut loose to see our friends and family. I hugged everyone tightly—my mother and Celestino, Daniela, and my two best friends from home, Emilio and Orlin. It felt like it had been years since I'd seen them.

My mom was giggly, jumping up and down. She squeezed me and laughed about my shaved head. The look in her eyes told me that she was proud of me, which told me that she was feeling better about my decision.

I strolled the grounds with my posse, introducing them to my friends, showing them landmarks. I ushered them by my bunk and locker, the chow hall, the latrines, even the phones where I'd hidden to call my mom.

As a group of us new soldiers walked out of the barracks, we practically ran head-on into one of our drill sergeants, Sergeant Lavalle. He was a white guy with a high-and-tight haircut, sarcastic and smart-assed but a professional soldier all the way through. He wished us well.

"Thank you, Drill Sergeant," one of the privates said, using the term we'd been instructed to use three months earlier.

"Don't call me 'Drill Sergeant' anymore. Now I'm just Sergeant Lavalle." As he began to walk away he turned and added, "But don't call me by my first name, or I'll smoke your asses."

I knew I couldn't let this one go by. "Thanks for everything," I said. "I'll never forget this experience, *Gregory*." He stepped toward me and I dodged away.

Later, my family and friends and I all piled into the car to head back to Dalton. I was going home for an entire month before I had to report to Fort Campbell, Kentucky. I was ready for some time off to relax and regroup.

Sadly, my first order of business was breaking up with Daniela. She had been a good girlfriend and I felt guilty, but I didn't know how we could continue to keep up a long-distance relationship when I was stationed at Fort Campbell, and I couldn't pretend anymore.

Being single again gave me lots of time to hang out with my boys. In the evenings, we went to the bowling alley and high school basketball games. We cruised around Dalton and drove up to a town in Tennessee called Cleveland, where guys would go to show off their cars.

My days were spent working at the recruiter's office. I'd go with him to speak to other kids about my experience. That was my first stab at public speaking, and it was good practice. I'd talk about the Army and how it wasn't as bad as I'd thought it'd be. "They toughen you up and you get through it," I'd say.

I wasn't spending a lot of time watching the evening news, but if I had, I'd have seen the potential for U.S. action in Iraq. Despite clear signs to the contrary, I still didn't think I'd be going anywhere soon. I was much too busy enjoying the prime of my life—fit, fresh out of basic training with a truckload of new confidence, and a bright career in the Army. I chose to focus on making the most of time off, not thinking too much about what lay ahead.

Before I knew it, it was time to ship off to Fort

Campbell, a four-hour drive northwest of Dalton and home to the 101st Airborne. PJ and a handful of other guys from basic were stationed there as well.

We were there for a few days before we were assigned to our units. We started every day with PT, physical training, which made me sore. I had quickly gotten out of shape lounging around at home the previous month.

Finally, I got my orders: I would be a member of the 502nd Infantry Regiment, Delta Company. I was bummed to learn that PJ was being sent to a different platoon. We lived in the same barracks, though, so we were still able to hang out.

Besides PJ, my team leader, Sergeant Christopher Valdez, probably was the most important person to me at Fort Campbell. At twenty-five, he was closer to my age than some of the other leaders, and you could tell he really cared about his guys. He'd already served in Kosovo, and he was a calm, collected person—a natural leader. I considered him a big brother.

I'd brought my cockiness from basic training with me to Fort Campbell, so Valdez made it his business to help me out and shut me up. I got a lot of hands-on from him, and I appreciated his attention. I had a lot to learn, and between Valdez and our platoon sergeant, Terrence O'Shea, I managed to stay out of big trouble and learn from these professionals.

A couple of weeks after I'd been placed in my unit, O'Shea gathered the platoon together.

"You *will* be deploying," he said, echoing what we'd been told at the end of basic. "Get yourselves mentally ready," he said.

I blew it off. I was still focused on having fun.

We had free time after work, with few restrictions and no curfew. At night we'd sample from the menu of Fort Campbell's finer off-base establishments. Unfortunately, most of those venues were out of reach to many of us because we weren't twenty-one, so we ended up most nights at an eighteen-and-over club called the Lighthouse, which had pool tables, a lounge area, and a dance floor. I loved to dance, and I always worked myself right into the middle of the floor. Although there were at least two guys for every girl, I still did all right.

Those of us who weren't legally permitted to drink alcohol got a big black X stamped onto our hands at the door. That really bugged my friends, who wished they could have a couple of drinks. But me, I never needed alcohol to enjoy myself.

There was only one time when that damned X turned against me. I was out there doing my moves when I made eye contact with a gorgeous girl on the edge of the floor. She didn't have an X on her hand. She wasn't quite cougar material, but she definitely had a couple of years on me. I motioned her over, and we hit the floor together. It was like a scene from a movie—we were all over each other, she was whipping her hair, I was touching her. I knew that she liked me. Everyone was looking at me like, "You got a hot older chick"—not older like a grandma, but a really hot chick. I got some respect for that.

I didn't want her to see my X, so I kept up the crazy dancing, trying to shield my flapping hands from her. It didn't work. She caught sight of the X and asked me how old I was.

"How old do you think I am?"

Okay, I'll admit it, stupid question. Finally I confessed I was nineteen, and that was all she wrote. I never saw her again after that night.

And then, in early February, a group of us were sitting in our company area when O'Shea came in. He walked to each man and handed him an envelope—our deployment orders.

I thought back to the recruiter's office in Dalton. After I'd finished filling out the enlistment documents, the recruiter asked my mom, "Ma'am, do you have any questions?"

She thought for a second, then said, "In case there is a war, you're not going to send him too soon, right?"

He looked her in the eyes. "Depends," he said. "But it's not too likely. There are a lot of soldiers who have been in the service for a while, and they would be the first to go."

I could see she was relieved.

But here in my hand, less than a year later, I held my orders. I turned the envelope over a few times and then took a deep breath. I pulled out the slip of paper.

We were going to the Middle East.

CHAPTER SEVEN

The Crucible

After several excruciating weeks of waiting, on March 8, 2003, we finally got word that we'd be shipping out within twenty-four hours. First stop, the staging area in Kuwait, and then on to the war zone in Iraq.

During the anxious days before, I had taken my personal stuff home to Dalton to store at our apartment. And I stayed in regular touch with my mom by phone, often several times a day, telling her, "Not today. Not today." Many times I'd drive all the way home just to spend the afternoon there.

After we received our orders, I dialed the familiar number in Dalton.

"Mom, it's time. We're going in the morning."

That evening, most soldiers were permitted to spend time with their families, so my mom and Celestino drove the 225-plus miles from Dalton up to Fort Campbell to see me off. We went to dinner at a Shoney's in nearby Hopkinsville and then over to Nashville for a carriage ride around the city. Just a regular night out with the family, as though nothing unusual were about to happen. But it was.

I deployed with the 2nd Brigade and the 502nd Infantry Regiment, 101st Airborne Division (Air Assault) out of Fort Campbell. I was one among approximately 150,000 U.S. troops sent to Iraq for the initial invasion, which would begin ten days later. Paramilitary teams had been inside Iraq since the previous summer, doing reconnaissance to identify senior Iraqi leaders for later targeting and persuading Iraqi military officers to surrender before the fighting began.

We were called to formation at 4 a.m. Afterward, I packed the rest of my stuff for my mother to take back to Dalton. The other soldiers' families began flooding onto the base to say goodbye. There is perhaps nothing more wrenching than a deployment farewell. Imagine the most tearful goodbye you've ever said to a loved one, then multiply it by a thousand.

When our sergeant gave the order for the soldiers to line up to board the buses, my mom started crying. I wanted her to believe I was okay, so I held in my own tears. I pulled her in for a hug, and we stayed like that for a long time. I leaned back and wiped at her tears with my thumb.

"Don't cry," I told her. "One way or another, I'm going to come back home. They can't stop me. I love you."

She reached into her bag and pulled out a small box. She placed it in my palm. Inside was a mariner's cross—a stylized version of a cross with the Christ figure atop a ship's anchor and wheel—hanging from a thin gold rope chain. It is traditionally given to sailors as a symbol of protection. I put it on, comforted by its feeling against my chest. Overseas, I would often pull it out of my shirt and kiss it.

"Be careful, mijo. I love you, too." My mom made the sign of the cross over me.

I boarded the bus and took a window seat. As we headed out toward the airfield, I craned my neck to watch my mother and Celestino until they were specks.

By the time I'd turned my gaze forward again, I'd compartmentalized my feelings. The crying and goodbyes were over. I was ready to do what I was trained to do.

The flight on a chartered jet to our staging ground in Kuwait, including a stopover in Rome to refuel, took eighteen hours. The distance between home and the oil-rich country of Kuwait, on the northwestern shore of the Persian Gulf, was more than seven thousand miles, but to me it might as well have been seven billion.

The desert landscape of this tiny nation—one of the smallest on the planet, with a population of fewer than three million souls—was completely alien to a boy from the American South. To me, the flat, sandy Arabian Desert, which covers most of the country, looked like the moon. The frequent sandstorms were unreal. We'd be walking to the dining facility when we'd see way off in the distance a swirl of sand. Moments later, the wind would pick up and start tossing around pebbles and earth. We had to put on our protective goggles, which made us look like ninjas.

I'd certainly seen poverty in El Salvador, so that element didn't surprise me. But the cultural differences were conspicuous. One of the first things I saw after touchdown in Kuwait was a woman squatting on the side of the road, peeing. She saw us curiously checking her out, and she didn't seem to care.

I also was struck by the emptiness, all these people living out in the middle of nowhere. There was no feeling of cohesiveness in the communities, no sense of this being anyone's home.

We bided our time in Kuwait at a camp called New York—others stayed in Camps Pennsylvania and New Jersey—while we waited for orders and equipment. We trained every day, which included lots of PT, time on the firing range, and briefing sessions about what to expect once we got inside enemy territory. Our lieutenant showed us a map of Iraq, pointing out population summaries and information about enemy forces. He briefed us on the locations and responsibilities of friendly units. He told us what we could expect from enemy efforts and how to be on the alert for saboteurs. He particularly noted the enemy's favorite tactics: ambush and mining the routes of transportation.

As a private I was the low man on the totem pole. I did the sorts of jobs no one else wanted to do. If trash needed to be dumped, I dumped it. If someone needed something, I fetched it. I got ammo for other soldiers, reloaded weapons as ordered. But I did these jobs with that little nerve that wanted to see action always twitching in the back of my mind.

At night we'd take to our twenty-man tents and hit the cots hard, mentally and physically exhausted. But then the warning siren would wail, piercing our ears and unnerving the hell out of us. We had to jump up, grab our weapons, pull on our gas masks, run to the defensive position inside the bunker, and wait for clearance. This happened frequently, so sleep deprivation was quickly added to the growing list of challenges.

But fatigue and fear of attack were no match for my propensity for getting into the usual trouble, courtesy of my big mouth.

Most soldiers, especially lower-ranking troops like myself, carried an M-16, a lightweight assault rifle, which had been standard issue since the Vietnam War. Lucky me, I found myself stuck with a weapon called an M249 light machine gun, also known as a Squad Automatic Weapon (SAW). There was nothing light about it. It weighed seventeen pounds empty and twenty-two pounds loaded, more than twice as heavy as the M-16. The soldier who usually carried this weapon hadn't yet reached the unit. I was assigned his piece until he arrived to claim it.

It wouldn't have been a big deal except that training meant running with much of our gear, and running with the M249 was like hauling a camel through the sand. I invariably fell behind the group.

"Hurry up, Martinez! Catch up, soldier!" Sergeant O'Shea would yell.

During one particularly brutal run, my anger bubbled up through my sweat. "It's bullshit that we're running in this heat!" Little did I know that we were enjoying what passes for spring in that part of the world, where high temperatures were merely in the high eighties; come summer, the high would soar another thirty-five degrees or more.

O'Shea didn't like my griping. "Get your soldier in line before I smoke his ass!" he hollered at Sergeant Valdez.

"Calm down, Martinez!" Valdez yelled at me in turn. "And shut your trap!"

I knew that refusing to behave could result in an Article 15, a nonjudicial punishment that permits commanders to mete out discipline without a court-martial. This write-up can range from a mere reprimand to a demotion and a dock in pay.

It's usually placed in your service record and can make it difficult for you to climb the rank ladder.

As much as I wanted to steer clear of an Article 15, the truth is I had opinions and questions. I didn't feel I was entitled to answers, but I wanted more direction instead of orders. But my superiors didn't take kindly to an expressive nineteen-year-old. The consequences were swift and sure: push-ups, sit-ups, extra runs, and, worst of all, long-winded lectures.

My mouth often got me into trouble with my peers as well. One evening while one of my platoon mates was changing his shirt, I saw that he was tattooed across the chest with our unit crest, an eagle's talon with the word *strike* below it.

I wondered aloud why someone would tattoo the symbol of his unit on his body.

With great restraint, he told me that our unit was a brotherhood and he was proud of it.

"I'd never get that tattooed on my body, because this isn't a brotherhood!" I said.

Our lieutenant overheard me. Oops.

As he smoked me outside, he reminded me that our unit indeed was a brotherhood. At that moment I realized what he was saying: We were at war, not running around in the Georgia woods playing Army. At the end of the day, we had to be able to count on each other to get ourselves back home. That is a brotherhood.

After about two weeks in Kuwait, our vehicles and equipment arrived. We were ready to drive our trucks across the border into Iraq. We were exhausted from the heat, from waiting, but we were unified in our desire to get in there and do our job.

Before we left, our commanders told us what would go down if we took casualties. If something happened to a guy, we shouldn't rush right in to give him aid, because we could be entering an ambush. Of course the Army doesn't advocate abandoning fallen comrades, but we needed to follow a procedure so we didn't jeopardize the mission and cause additional casualties.

But to me, it was black and white. I said, "Bullshit. There's no way I'm leaving anybody behind." I found myself doing push-ups for that one. The Army didn't need me to tell them how to run their operation.

We were warned to distrust all Iraqis. Rumors flew about women being sent forward to consort with the troops to get inside information and insurgents strapping explosives to children.

"If a child comes up to your truck, don't stop, no matter what," they told us.

"What, we're just supposed to keep going?"

"Just nudge them out of the way and keep going."

How could I do that? I wondered.

We'd all been trained to spot land mines and

roadside bombs, but they blended pretty well with the terrain. They were like the bogeyman—you knew they were out there waiting to get you, but you didn't know where or when.

Driving along, we'd frequently encounter Iraqi locals walking alongside the road. We'd nod and pass by. Sometimes the inevitable happened: After a few minutes, we'd hear *kaboom!* The pedestrian we'd just passed had triggered a mine. Occasionally we'd cruise past bodies and body parts—land mine victims all.

I remember one specific occasion when we passed a lone woman on foot. Her black abaya slapped at the ground, revealing her worn black sandals. Ten minutes later I heard the explosion. I wondered, *How could you be there one minute, walking with a purpose, your sons and daughters waiting for you at home, and then the next minute you don't exist?* The sound of that explosion haunted me.

The George W. Bush administration launched Operation Iraqi Freedom with several objectives: end the despotic regime of Saddam Hussein, which purportedly was allied with Al Qaeda; locate weapons of mass destruction (the existence of which was later found to be grossly exaggerated); secure the infrastructure and populace; and eventually assist in rebuilding the country and establishing a representative government.

The invasion north from Kuwait through

Hillah and Najaf would move on to Karbala and finally to Baghdad and then Mosul in the far north. Our division attacked through the entire country from south to north, conducting two of the longest air assaults in history back-to-back. The 3rd Infantry Division, the first conventional U.S. unit to enter Baghdad during the 2003 invasion, had basically bypassed the city of Karbala, about sixty miles southwest of Baghdad, in their race to the capital, so the city hadn't been secured. The mission of the 2nd Brigade was to clear Karbala.

In early April, my company received its orders: We were to clear routes and provide external and perimeter security while our units approached Karbala. It was a two-day fight to seize the city, incorporating ten battalions and around six thousand soldiers.

Just a couple of days earlier, Jessica Lynch, an Army supply clerk from West Virginia, had been snatched back from the hands of Iraqis after her convoy had been attacked. She and a dozen other soldiers had been taken hostage. Lynch was the first American POW since World War II to be rescued (although in the months to follow it was revealed that the rescue was dramatized as more of a PR stunt than a rescue, since the enemy had fled the hospital where she was being kept before our forces swept in under the cloak of darkness to grab her). Eight members of her company weren't as lucky—their bodies were recovered at the time of Lynch's rescue.

April 5 started at the miserable hour of 4 a.m. Stumbling around groggy, I gathered my gear, muttering, "This sucks." We members of the 502nd Infantry Regiment, Delta Company, brushed our teeth, emptied our bladders, and put on our gear.

Less than a month in the war zone, I had already reached the point where I was looking forward to seeing action. Plenty of times our sergeant had summoned us to explain our mission, and the other guys and I would tell each other, "Okay, now we're getting into the real shit." Then twenty minutes later we'd be told to stand down, that the assignment had been canceled or that it had been given to another unit. When we actually went out on the missions, they weren't what they were cracked up to be.

Many of us younger soldiers didn't understand what we were doing in this war, thousands of miles from home. But when we were handed a mission, we always got worked up because inactivity could be so boring.

Tasked with providing security for other military groups as they traveled through war-torn Iraq, this morning we found ourselves escorting an enormous convoy of about ninety trucks. I was in my HMMWV—a High Mobility Multi-purpose Wheeled Vehicle, or Humvee—along with three other soldiers: Justin Hart, Joshua

Hopkins, and Ernest Clayton. The vehicle was equipped with cloth doors and basic armor around a weapon mount on the roof. There was no air-conditioning to relieve us from the searing heat, the kind of heat that causes the landscape to ripple in the distance.

Every time the group came to a halt, we all dismounted, observed the area, and waited for the next order. At some point we were told that we couldn't travel along the road we'd originally been on, so we pulled off and three of the four of us got out to pull security. I was already exhausted from lack of sleep, and the sun zapped every last reserve of my stamina. Standing upright with my weapon, I dozed off for a couple of minutes.

I was startled awake by Hopkins, our truck commander, or TC.

"Martinez, it's your turn to drive!"

His permanent position was in the front passenger seat, and he called the shots. Out of the four guys in the hummer, only two of us rotated the driving.

I'd developed a hatred of driving since we'd gotten to Iraq. It seemed I was always picked to drive when we were either going out or returning to camp late at night. In the pitch black, with helmet-mounted night vision goggles our only resource, I found it harrowing to try to propel a wide truck down a dark road. The stress is intense on the eyes and you can't see anything clearly.

Sometimes I would fall off the trail because I couldn't see. A few times I got the Humvee stuck in a ditch, and we had to be pulled out. Sergeant O'Shea wasn't amused, and frankly neither was I—all those missteps made me feel like a failure.

But at the TC's instruction, I took the wheel.

Near 11 a.m. we received our second set of orders for the day, modifying our original mission. We were directed to pull security around Karbala while we waited for our command to decide the next move.

We pulled up into a staging area, and Hart got into a firing position behind his .50-cal. Clayton, Hopkins, and I dismounted to pull security. We were parked for about forty minutes. More than the whole platoon was there, about seventy-five soldiers, but our vehicles were separated in case of enemy contact. Stinging sweat poured into my eyes.

Then we received orders to push on along a route that hadn't been cleared. This wasn't an uncommon scenario at this stage of the game. We didn't always have route-clearance teams and other explosive ordnance or engineer support. Units were required to clear on the move or, as we said, conduct in-stride breaches. This practice included firing .50-caliber rounds into berms and using bangalore torpedoes and other explosives. It didn't seem like a great idea. I complained about it, and I heard others, including

Sergeant Valdez, doing the same. But with no choice about the matter, we shoved the thought to the back of our minds and moved on.

When American troops first took Baghdad, only our military police had fully armored vehicles, so combat soldiers would line the floorboards of their Humvees with sandbags to deflect blasts and repel bomb fragments. That's how our unit outfitted our vehicles. Other units improvised armor for themselves out of scrap metal, calling it "hillbilly armor" or "hajji armor." By August the Army would begin deploying "up-armor" kits that included ballistic windows and fully integrated armor to better protect military vehicles. But on that day in April, there wasn't much more than a pile of sandbags on the floorboards between us and the enemy.

I was ordered to move up to the lead group of the convoy. I sighed and pushed on the accelerator, driving the Humvee with one hand on the wheel and the other on the center console, like I was tooling around in my own car back home. Someone made a joke, and I remember laughing through my irritation. I turned onto a concrete road, following closely behind Sergeant Valdez in the Humvee directly in front of me.

BOOM!

My left front tire made contact with a roadside bomb.

The sound crashed through my ears to my

brain, banging it against either side of my skull. A pressurized blast wave unfurled outward at a pace of hundreds of meters per second. A secondary wind followed—a huge volume of displaced air flooding back into the vacuum—pounding me with debris. I felt the waves at my feet and then as they quivered up my body.

The heat from the explosion roared into a fire that sounded oddly like falling rain. Within seconds, my vehicle was almost completely consumed by fire. Rounds from the stored ammo in the vehicle were going off. I watched as the flames licked up from the floor and my hands started to burn, the skin melting away. The blaze reached my face, and with great effort I pulled up my seared hands—like paws now—to try to shield myself. I got a taste of sweetness on my tongue—perhaps a physiological reaction to the blast. The oxygen burned up in the fire, and I struggled to breathe. I was frantic with pain and terror.

I'm going to die, I thought.

Somewhere outside I heard our .50-cal rounds cooking off. It made me think of Fourth of July fireworks.

In all the war movies I'd seen since I was a kid, whenever soldiers were blown up, it seemed to happen lightning fast. But in real life the clock eased almost to a halt, and I was able to process everything that was happening to me.

I watched my dreams fade away as my nineteen-year-old life rewound. I saw myself as a little boy with my mom. I saw my mom at my grave. Her head bowed, covered with a mantilla; she was crying. A soldier passed her the triangle of American flag. I knew that my mother would be ruined. And then I reflected on a couple of pretty trivial truths: All the girls I wanted to date would move on. The NFL would find talent in some other kid. I wouldn't get the chance to have all the adventures guaranteed a young man.

As if in answer, a young girl appeared. It was the same child my mom had once shown me in a black-and-white photo, but this girl before me now was a teenager. She was wearing a pink dress with long sleeves and ruffles. I'd never met my late sister, Anabel, but I knew this was her. When she appeared, the chaos and noise around me faded.

"You're going to be okay," she told me. "Mom needs you."

I don't remember what her voice sounded like or even whether she spoke in English or Spanish, but I heard her. Then, as quickly as she had entered my life, she disappeared.

Valdez and O'Shea ran to my burning Humvee. One of our antitank missiles exploded from the rack, kicking the sergeants back against a nearby wall. I had been ejected from the vehicle and was sitting about two feet from the Humvee. Once they recovered, Valdez and O'Shea grabbed my forearms, but some of my uniform and skin came off in their hands, so they reached behind my back to drag me away by my body armor.

The two men, assisted by Clayton, hauled me to the rear of O'Shea's Humvee, which was a troop carrier. They dumped me into the back. As O' Shea took stock of the casualties, he told Valdez to help me find my "happy place," so I could win the psychological battle of staying alive. Valdez got into the Humvee with me. He drew my head into his lap. I was in shock, so he began to rock me, calling me "baby boy," repeating that he wasn't going to leave me. "You're going to be okay," he said.

I sensed it wasn't true. I struggled to get air.

"Try to breathe through your nose," he said.

Up front, O'Shea attempted to call for a medevac as we sped toward the emergency casualty evacuation site.

I reached up to touch my face, but Valdez knocked my hands down. My uniform had melted into my skin. I clawed at his neck. When we reached the casevac, two frontline ambulances were waiting. Valdez helped the medical team hoist me onto a litter and watched anxiously while they tried to clear my airway.

Parts of my swollen face were scorched black. My hands were burned and my head was bleeding. Blood was leaking from my ears. The medics attempted to remove my clothing so they could put the burn blankets on me to try to cool the skin and stop the burn progression.

"I want to go home!" I screamed. "I want to go home! I want to go home!"

The medics tried to insert a breathing tube down my throat, but I was out of my mind with fear and pain, and I fought them like they were the enemy.

I reached toward Valdez. "Please don't leave me!"

I wondered how much the human body is able to withstand before it shuts off. I had such plans —to play football, to go to college. Now I wondered, *Would I make it? Would my mother be okay? Would I be remembered? How the hell did I get here?*

Through my own screams I heard the familiar low thump and felt the merciful cold wind of a Black Hawk helicopter.

CHAPTER EIGHT

Twilight

Back in Georgia, my mom stifled a yawn. It was six thirty in the morning, promising to be a bright spring day, and her twelve-hour shift at the Shaw carpet plant would be over in a few hours. Her job—replacing bobbins of yarn in the carpet-binding machine—was repetitive, calming, meditative. At a neighboring machine, her coworkers Nora and Jesus bantered and laughed. Mom laughed, too, but inside she was thinking about me, her only son, wondering how I was, on the other side of the world in a war zone.

Whenever the phone rang in the office, it reverberated through the entire plant. This time when it rang, my mother didn't hear it. She happened to raise her head and spotted her boss, Raul, heading toward her. He was smiling, but she thought his smile didn't look right. *Please don't let him be coming to me,* she prayed. But he was.

"Hey, Maria, let's go to my office," he said. She felt her heart jump in her chest.

"What did I do?" she joked weakly.

In the office, she saw the phone was off the

hook, lying on the desk. Raul stepped back. "You have a call," he said, and she knew. With a shaking hand, she picked up the receiver.

"Hello?"

"Is this Maria Zavala?" a voice asked. Before she could answer, the caller introduced himself and said, "Are you Private Martinez's mother?"

She tried to answer but at first nothing came out. Then she said, "What happened to my son?"

There had been an accident the day before, the caller told her. A land mine.

"Tell me what happened to my son!" she repeated. "Is he alive?"

"Your son is not dead," the caller answered. "We got him breathing. Let me give you a phone number so you can get more information."

Her eyes met Raul's, and she handed the receiver to him. He took down a name and a number with a Washington, D.C., area code. My mom's quiet tears dissolved into muffled sobs. *My son isn't going to make it,* she thought. *And if he doesn't, I won't.* Everyone at work knew it—if my mom lost me, they'd lose her. If anyone took me away from her, she had no reason to continue.

She always told people that I was her doctor, her pastor, her therapist, and her entertainer. "Mama, everything's going to be okay," I'd tell her when I was little and she was sad. "Someday I'm going to grow up and take care of you and there will be no more tears."

She had driven my car to work that day and she wanted to drive herself home in it, wrapped in something of mine as though it were my arms holding her in an embrace. But her coworkers insisted on giving her a ride.

In her apartment, Mom headed to the small shrine where she regularly prayed. She grasped an eight-by-ten rendering of the Niño de Atocha and put its face to her stomach.

"Why aren't you taking care of J.R.?" she asked it.

She promised the Niño she wouldn't let go of the image until I was okay. Then she sank onto the couch and wept, as her friends from the plant began to arrive to offer their support. As their shifts ended, more people came by to sit with her.

The Pentagon didn't have many answers. It was too soon to know much. They told her that I had been treated at the 212th MASH and transferred to the 47th Combat Support Hospital. From there I'd been evacuated to Landstuhl Regional Medical Center, which was not only the largest military hospital but also the only top-level military trauma center outside the United States. Nearly all military personnel wounded in Afghanistan and Iraq were sent there. They assured my mom I'd receive the finest care.

The next morning my mom began to call again, dialing that number in D.C. and new numbers she'd been given for Fort Campbell. She spoke to a surgeon who told her to write down her questions for my doctor in Germany so she'd remember what to ask when she was connected.

Finally, she was patched over to Germany. My doctor at Landstuhl told her they were preparing to transfer me back to the United States. I would end up at Brooke Army Medical Center in San Antonio. Named after Brigadier General Roger Brooke, who commanded the center from 1929 to 1933 and introduced the use of routine diagnostic chest X-rays, the sprawling, 425-bed state-of-the-art facility also houses the Department of Defense's trailblazing burn injury facility.

"So you're saying my son is going to live?"

Yes, the doctor told her. "But his prognosis depends on the severity of the damage to his lungs." I'd sustained a severe inhalation injury from the heat and smoke of the fire that consumed the Humvee I'd been driving. The doctors planned to conduct exploratory abdominal surgery to check the scope of the internal damage.

"Also, he has severe burns over one-third of his body."

My mom wanted to go to Germany to be with me. If I were that close to death, she reasoned, it would help me to see her—even just hear her voice. But the doctor said no, and that "no" actually gave her hope. It meant I wasn't going to die.

"Don't worry," the doc said. "He's in my hands, and he's going to make it."

A thousand miles west of Dalton, Sergeant First Class Robert Mazak's government-issued cell phone buzzed in his pocket. The forty-year-old physical therapy technician, a soldier himself and a father of three, was part of a critical-care air transport team out of the burn unit at Brooke Army Medical Center. As the operations non-commissioned officer for the team, Mazak took care of everything but the patients on flights out of Landstuhl to BAMC. Since the war had begun a month earlier, Mazak found himself on an airplane several times a week.

As usual, Colonel Dave Barillo, one of the unit's surgeons, was on the other end of the phone. "Spin up the team," he told Mazak. "We've got another soldier to bring home."

Mazak got to work. He reached out to the burn flight team (BFT) on call, which included a burn surgeon, a respiratory therapist, a burn intensive-care nurse, other RNs and LVNs, and a burn flight physician's assistant. Then he called the operations center to process the commercial flight arrangements to carry them to Germany.

When the team had assembled, they checked the prestaged equipment and supplies they would bring on their flight to Germany—the pumps, monitors, respirators, ventilators—everything you'd see in a burn intensive-care unit. Within about three hours from Barillo's call, the BFT members were settled in their seats for the twelve-hour flight to Frankfurt.

Back at Landstuhl, the medical team was getting me ready. They'd charted my injuries, which were varied and many. I had 34 percent total body surface-area burns—with 10 percent second-degree and 24 percent third-degree. I had bilateral corneal abrasions and ulcerations. Nasal, head, rib, and shoulder fractures. Grade III liver laceration. A ruptured eardrum.

I was losing a lot of my vital body fluids through my large, open burn areas, so the medical team rehydrated me with additional fluids. They injected sedatives and narcotics to keep me calm and pain-free. They conducted numerous blood tests to determine how my body was reacting to my injuries, and they infused lifesaving medicines into me. The respiratory therapists were busy checking and maintaining proper oxygen and breathing parameters.

Mazak spent his time on the flight going over every detail in his flight log—the timeline for the patient, orders given, decisions made—and tried to doze. The BFT landed in Frankfurt the following morning. They loaded all their gear—fifteen large cases—into Army vehicles sent by Landstuhl and began the two-hour ride to the base.

Their focus would be to stabilize me for transport back to the United States. If a patient's condition is too precarious, the team won't take him or her but instead will stay in Germany to provide care until the patient is stable enough to be transferred. Medical personnel would make every effort to get every service member back to the United States. As the war progressed, it became obvious that some of the injured troops weren't going to survive. The transport teams honored a second unspoken mission: If they couldn't get someone home with the expectation of survival and recovery, then it was equally important to get that patient home so that he or she would die in the United States instead of a foreign country, and to provide the family the opportunity to say goodbye.

Once at the hospital, the BAMC team began to work on me. They removed all the dressings and assessed me. They cleaned my wounds and reapplied bandages, then placed me on a padded stretcher. All my medical equipment—ventilators, pumps, monitors, IV bags, and oxygen tanks—was attached to the stretcher, which was transformed into a mini-ICU.

The team loaded me and a couple of other patients onto a bus and we rolled to Ramstein Air Base, where we boarded a military transport plane headed for the other side of the world. The patients didn't so much board as we were stacked like trays of pies in a bakery, so that we could be more easily monitored.

During the flight, the team was busy checking and adjusting medications and oxygen levels and ensuring that staff documented all the proper medical information. Mazak updated his flight diary and saw that everyone had meals and drinks for the long flight back. Then he made his way forward to the cockpit, where he was patched through to the burn unit to update the waiting team. The contact on the ground in San Antonio reminded the ambulance company to be at the airport for pickup—one ambulance for each patient—and contacted the ICUs and the wards to make sure everyone would be prepared.

The aircraft landed at the San Antonio airport on Wednesday, April 9, 2003, one month after I'd shipped out from Fort Campbell.

I don't remember any of this. Not a minute. I'd been intubated and sedated. I needed to be on the ventilator because my lungs weren't working well enough to support me, and the doctors kept me infused with narcotics and sedatives to keep me comfortable. It was like being under general anesthesia.

I wouldn't regain consciousness for three weeks.

It's humbling to know now that so many dedicated people had worked in tandem to get me out of Iraq and back onto U.S. soil still alive. All those people intent on saving my life, and I wasn't even aware of it. I was one of the very first combat patients from the Iraq War to enter the Brooke burn center. Although the Army Burn Center is one of the oldest and most experienced in the world, few of the staff at that point in time were old enough to have had firsthand experience with wartime burns and the center didn't have nearly the resources it has today. Their plan was to offer continuity of care, in which each patient would benefit by having the same doctors, nurses, and other staff throughout his or her stay at the hospital. They'd follow each patient from admittance to discharge, giving a lot of attention to patients and family members.

The day before I arrived, my mom took a call from the social worker on staff. "We're going to be receiving your son here," she said. It would be another sixteen hours before my mom got word that I was there.

My mom had wanted to be with me when I arrived in the United States.

"That's not how this works," the social worker told her. "If a transport plane is diverted or a patient becomes too ill to continue to the destination, the Army doesn't want to have the family waiting in the wrong location. So they wait to bring the family members until the patient actually checks into the facility."

The social worker told my mom that they'd arrange a flight for her leaving that afternoon at four thirty from Chattanooga, Tennessee, the closest metropolitan airport to Dalton. She packed her clothes and even packed some for me, reasoning that when I gave interviews to the media I'd need to look sharp. She knew I was badly hurt, but she didn't really accept it.

My mom was still clutching the picture of the Niño de Atocha to her body, like it was a real little boy, when she got on the plane.

At the airport in San Antonio, she was greeted by three hospital reps, who escorted her to BAMC. Her emotions were swinging wildly. While hours earlier she'd optimistically packed clothing for me to wear on television, now she visualized my funeral, imagined people holding clods of dirt to toss onto my casket, in which I was laid to rest dressed in my Class A uniform.

He's my pride, she thought. *If he doesn't make it, I have no more pride.*

The social worker met my mom as she stepped off the elevator in the burn unit. The two of them hurried down the corridor to my ICU room and stopped at the big picture window looking in. My body was covered with white dressings. Both of my arms were elevated in slings to minimize swelling and increase blood flow, my knees were slightly bent, and my head was raised. The staff called this position the "burn crucifix." I had a feeding tube in my nose, and my face was dark from open wounds and burned tissue. IV poles hung on either side of the bed with pumps attached, bags of fluids dangling above.

My mom burst into tears at the sight.

"It's okay," the social worker told her. "Cry now, as much as you want, and get it out. Once you walk into the room, you need to be finished crying. Even though he can't see you or talk, he might hear you and that could upset him."

That's why the picture window was a stopping point for visitors: It wasn't uncommon for them to dissolve into tears at the first sight of their wounded loved one. Most civilians are spared the sight of the horrific injuries that members of the military can receive in combat. The staff wanted to ensure that extreme emotional reactions occurred out of the patient's earshot. It was also better for the visitors to be in a location where the staff could help them recover.

After my mom pulled herself together, the nurses showed her how to put on the PPE, or personal protective equipment—shoe covers, gown, mask, and gloves. The final touch was winding her long black hair into the bonnet. They opened the door, and she went to my bed.

She looked at my face and arms and hands. My hands looked like someone had cut them with a knife. Her eyes gazed down to my feet.

"Is this your son?" the nurse asked her. How could a mother recognize her son? By his feet.

"Yes, that's him," she replied.

After a brief visit, they took my mom to the

nearby guesthouse, a temporary-housing facility where she'd stay for the next two months.

My mom asked for a room where she could see the hospital from the window. Every so often in the middle of the night she'd go to that window and look up at the lights, wondering what was going on in my room. Sometimes she wouldn't fall asleep until dawn, when it was time for her to get back up.

In the meantime, an extraordinary team of professionals cared for me. The burn center director, Dave Barillo, was attending me personally. Over the next months, Barillo's stocky frame was a frequent presence in my room, and if he wasn't looking at me, he was talking to my mom.

And Bonnie Jackson was the burn ICU's charge nurse. An academic with a calm demeanor, Jackson had seen burns of all types, severely disfigured and depressed patients, and distraught families. The average age of her combat patients was between twenty and thirty-five. She treated all of them like they were her own children. In fact, all of the ICU staff was very protective and possessive of the patients, and sometimes patients became more dependent on their nurses than on their parents or spouses.

Back in Dalton, word of my injury spread fast. Susan Ward heard it from one of her middle school students, and she got on the phone with Coach McClurg. He didn't know anything, but he began calling around and Susan began calling around, and between the two of them they learned that I'd been burned. Susan found BAMC on the Internet and called the facility.

"I need to know if you have this young man," she told the burn unit receptionist.

"I'm sorry, ma'am," he replied, "I can't give out that information."

Susan wasn't having any of that. "You don't understand," she said. "My husband is on staff at the high school, and this kid is one of ours. I need to know."

The receptionist turned her down again.

"Okay," Susan persisted. "If I ask you questions, can you answer yes or no?"

The receptionist said he might be able to do that.

"Do you have a Hispanic male from Georgia?"

"We might," he answered.

"Would his name be Jose Rene Martinez?" she asked.

"It might." Then the man gave Susan the phone number to the guesthouse where the patient's mother just might be staying.

Susan was the first of our friends who called to support us; many were people my mom had never met. When she'd get a call, she'd jot down the person's name, how he or she was connected to me, and a phone number. She kept this list to show me.

And by the first weekend, we had visitors. Jacob and Jeris—the other two-thirds of the

Multicultural Idiots—made the eight-hour drive with Jacob's mother. When my mom worried aloud about how I might end up looking, Jacob's mom made her laugh. "Don't you worry about that," she said. "He'll be fine. Look what they did with Michael Jackson." The next weekend my godmother, Alejandra, came from Louisiana. But the most important people—my grandmother and my sister, Consuelo—weren't there.

My mom begged the social worker to try to bring them up from El Salvador. The social worker wrote to the consulate and even obtained approval for the plane tickets, but in the end, someone in the Salvadoran consulate denied the request. My mother was crushed.

But friends in Hope and Dalton continued to rain down encouragement. Acquaintances and even strangers sent their good wishes. Schoolkids sent get-well cards. Coach Stubber called my mom from Hope nearly every night. He probably spoke to her forty-five days in a row, every day. "Maria, this is Coach," he'd say, and ask how I had done in the twenty-four hours since they'd last spoken. Stubber heard the determination in my mom's voice, but he heard the fear as well.

In those first days, even my doctor, Dave Barillo, was afraid for me. Just about anything and everything can go wrong with burn patients. Serious burns represent the most severe injury a person can suffer and still survive. Once the proportion of burned area rises above 20 percent, every organ in the body begins to work overtime. The heart pumps at two and a half times the normal rate. The immune system breaks down, so the patient is at great risk of infection. Burn patients aren't out of the woods until they go home. Barillo had seen patients survive for a year in the hospital and still die from some complication before going home.

And I wasn't simply a burn patient—I was a blast injury/overpressure injury/abdominal trauma patient with a 34 percent burn. I wasn't responding well to treatment and I became increasingly unstable as the days passed.

The inhalation injury, which is a chemical burn to the lungs and airways, was the biggest challenge to me in the first few weeks after the blast. In the fire I had inhaled air heated to 1,200 degrees as well as potentially more than three hundred toxins spewed from the burning vehicle, which made it difficult to get enough oxygen into the body. The smaller-particle toxins tend to end up in the lungs. The fix for that was to ventilate me and hope my lungs repaired themselves.

Finally, after two weeks, I began to turn around. In time I grew strong enough to breathe on my own. In another week, it would be time to wake me up.

One afternoon about ten days in, when I was still in my deep sleep, nurses asked me to respond if I could hear them. I moved a toe. My mom was ecstatic to hear the news. She rushed to my bedside and asked me to do it again. Nothing. Day after day, she tried again, and nothing.

By Sunday, April 14, my mom was feeling pretty dejected. She was just asking me for one little sign, and I wouldn't deliver. Before visiting hours she went to the chapel and then on to my room. It was noon. She leaned over my face, absorbing all of me, staring at my closed eyes.

"Mijo," she said, "I'm here." She chatted as she always did, like she was talking to a doll. She talked and talked. Nothing.

"*Mi amor*, I'm your mommy. If you hear me, give me a signal. Move your little feet."

My feet didn't move.

"Son, move your little eyes if you can hear me."

I squeezed my eyes.

Her prayers, and all the prayers of the people who had been rooting for me, had been answered.

"Mijo," she whispered, "do you remember Coach Stubber?"

I squeezed my eyes.

"Do you remember Jacob's mother?"

I squeezed again.

"Do you remember the Multicultural Idiots?"

Again.

"Do you remember Mucho?"

I answered with my eyes.

"Do you know that Mommy loves you very much?"

Squeeze.

"Do you love me?"

Nothing. I didn't respond.

She repeated the question: "Do you love your mom?"

Still nothing.

"It's okay," she assured me. "I love you anyway."

Those few minutes restored her faith, the faith that had been shattered sixteen years earlier by my sister's death. She decided to ask God for just a bit more. She sank to her knees on the floor of my hospital room. "God," she prayed, "if it's true that you exist in the blue sky, just take a little look through this window and make this child wake up."

Nothing.

Without another word, she got to her feet and left.

Back at the guesthouse she climbed into her bed, though it was only early afternoon, and considered what had just happened. Had God prompted her child to show her those signs? Yes, she decided, he had. She got out of bed and again went to her knees: She asked God to forgive her. "You know what you're doing, but I don't want to listen," she prayed. "Thank you for letting me have J.R. I'm letting you have the child you've already taken. Thank you for letting me keep this one."

My mom, wearing a dress she sewed for herself, and me at four months old, dressed up for a picture.

My father and mother with me at six months old. Bossier City, Louisiana.

Me at age two
with my mom.

Dressed up like a
cowboy, age three,
Bossier City,
Louisiana.
(This outfit did not
make me happy.)

Happy fourth
birthday!

First-grade school photo.

Eight years old, with my sister Consuelo, fourteen, El Salvador. We were embarrassed to pose for Mom's camera.

Trying on my first football uniform, age eleven.

My mom and me, age thirteen, in Louisiana.

Junior year, Hope High School, Hope, Arkansas.

Senior prom, spring 2002, in front of our apartment.

High school graduation: a proud moment for us both.

At my U.S. Army swearing-in ceremony. My friends Gabriel and Daniela flanking me on the left, with my mom and Celestino on the right.

Back from basic training and hanging out with friends (from left) Derek, Vanessa, and Emilio, December 2002.

A weekend at home in Dalton one week before deploying to Iraq, saluting before the Virgin Mary at church.

Displaying my head and chest expanders, July 2004.

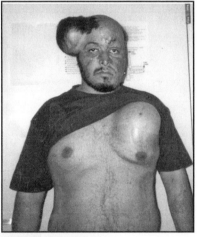

Brooke Army Medical Center, 2005, after doctors removed two expanders during a thirteen-hour surgery.

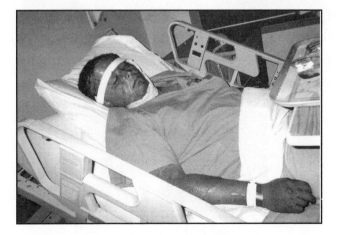

Me and Dan Vargas at a fundraiser for Operation Finally Home.

Speaking at a Memorial Day event in Los Angeles, 2010.

When I'd have downtime from *Dancing with the Stars*, Romeo always had to remind me of his place, 2011.

Me, Belle, and her proud grandmother, May 2012.

CHAPTER NINE

Who Will Love Me Now?

For three weeks I had lain in that bed, hovering somewhere between complete darkness and the most vivid of dreams. And then, through the fog, I heard a man's voice.

"Private Martinez," he said. "Private Martinez, if you can hear me, open your eyes."

I obeyed, but the bright lights hurt, and I slammed them shut again.

"It's okay to take your time," the voice said. "When you're ready, open them."

After a couple of seconds, I blinked again and focused slowly on the ceiling above me—white tiles with a swirly pattern.

"Private Martinez," the voice insisted. It was a little irritating. "Private Martinez, we're going to remove the tube. We need you to cough as much as possible, okay?"

I nodded. Something hard in my chest was dragged upward, through my throat and out my mouth. I gagged. They sat me up. I coughed and coughed, expelling all that stuff that had been sitting in my airway for weeks.

When I couldn't cough anymore, I sat limply like a baby while someone wiped the drool from my chin. I raised my head and stared in front of me at the sea of masked, bonneted people in green.

"Private Martinez." There he was again. "We have someone special here who's been by your side the whole time."

It was my mom, the person I loved most in the world. I allowed my head to roll to the right and was able to bring my gaze to meet hers. Her eyes were all that were visible. Like everyone else who came into my room, she was wearing PPE—a mask, surgical cap, gown, and gloves. But I could see her tears in her eyes. She touched my hand lightly.

"I love you, Mama," I croaked out, surprised to hear my own voice. It was hoarse—my vocal cords raw from the breathing tube.

The voice spoke again from somewhere over my bed. "You're in San Antonio, Texas," he told me.

What was I doing in Texas? Last time I checked, I'd been in Iraq. "What the hell am I doing in San Antonio?" I said aloud.

I heard a round of appreciative laughter. Dr. Barillo introduced himself and explained that I'd been injured in Iraq and that I was being treated in the burn unit at Brooke Army Medical Center. He asked me if I remembered what had happened. I nodded, but he explained anyway—that I'd run over a mine and been burned. I listened politely but felt really tired.

Before I drifted back to sleep, I turned to my mom. "I told you I was going to come back home."

Later, when I was fully awake, I told my mom about the vision I'd had of the teenage girl who said, "You're going to be okay. Mom needs you."

She and I murmured "Anabelita" almost at the same moment.

My mom reminded me that when I'd visited Anabel's burial site in El Salvador, I'd sobbed and sobbed and didn't want to leave the grave. That had broken her heart, and she'd wondered about this link between me and the sister I'd never met.

"She's been watching over you," my mom said now.

"You mean like my guardian angel?"

"Yes, mijo," she answered.

That made perfect sense. I'd always felt that Anabel and I had a special connection. Now I had proof.

The next day Dr. Barillo was in my room again. He pulled over a chair and sat next to my bed so I could see him without moving my head.

"Right now you can't do much for yourself because of your injuries," he said, "so a nurse will be taking care of you." He explained that my nurse would come in every morning at seven thirty or so and feed me. Then my nurse would put me on a shower bed—a rolling waterproof tray—and push me into the shower room to bathe me.

The doctor talked about all the other tasks that

the nurse would do for me, but after a bit I tuned him out. I could hear his voice, but in my mind I began to create my own story line starring this nurse. I imagined this angel of mercy as a beautiful young girl, about twenty-two, just out of college. I'd never really had a "type," but this girl would be a blonde with beautiful light eyes—green or blue—and a Coke-bottle figure. There would be instant attraction between the two of us, which she'd try to conceal. But I'd see it in her smile, the way her eyes would close when I'd make her laugh. We'd fall in love. We'd close the door to my room and make out. I'd be released from the hospital as good as new, and I'd marry this gorgeous woman and we'd have kids together. My mom would be so happy, and so would we.

And then I heard another voice say, "Hi, I'm Mike. I'm your nurse."

Mike Shiels was a tall thirty-year-old Irishman whose nose crinkled when he smiled, although at the time I could only see his blue eyes. His long hair was collected under his bonnet and his goatee was hidden beneath his surgical mask.

"You're not my nurse," I sputtered. No way.

"What were you expecting?" he asked.

"A girl," I said.

Mike laughed. "Don't they all?"

I was crushed. I thought about how this Mike guy would be feeding me like a baby and bathing me, of all things. The idea of this guy touching me like that—well, that would be embarrassment on top of indignity. But he'd been a licensed vocational nurse, or LVN, for ten years. He liked to say that, as a medical professional, "You either love burns or you can't handle them." He definitely fell into the former camp. Caring for someone like me was personal for him. I was a soldier, and he'd been a soldier, so we understood each other.

And as a nurse, his job was to keep patients alive and get them out of BAMC. He never felt sorry for me, because he knew he was starting me on a long journey and that eventually he'd see me getting out of bed and living my life. His confidence flowed into me and made me feel, more often than not, that I wasn't a victim.

But my pain was constant, despite the pain medication—often methadone—that Mike and the other nurses administered. Burn pain, I've since heard, is like no other. In addition to the agony caused by tissue destruction, burn injury invites further torment by stimulating inflammation and hyperalgesia, an extreme sensitivity to painful stimuli. Irritating substances aggravate the exposed nerve endings, packing an even bigger punch.

My weeks in the burn ICU became routine. Most mornings—when he was on duty—a cheerful, energetic Mike would wake me up. He gave me some time to rouse myself while he went back out to get my breakfast. As I awaited his return, I'd try to grab a few more minutes of sleep, like a middle school kid, before the day started.

When he returned, he clicked on the TV, usually ESPN, and we'd talk about sports—the Spurs, the NBA playoffs—while he fed me, holding the spoon to my mouth because my hands were "frozen" into closed claws.

After breakfast, Mike reviewed the plan of the day and discussed our goals and timeline. I'd state my concerns and Mike would answer my questions. I'd ask him why he did certain things, and he'd explain. He always spelled out everything he planned to do so I'd be mentally prepared for each move. But the morning shower was one element of daily care that defied preparation.

Mike and an assistant would load me onto a shower bed and wheel me down the hall, ceiling lights blinking past. The shower room, called the tank, was kept at a temperature of 100 degrees. Skin keeps us warm, so a burned person with compromised skin can't maintain body temperature and isn't able to insulate himself. The place smelled like pure hospital with a dollop of burned skin. Mike would direct the shower-head onto my body; in some places I could perceive the sensation of the water, in other areas I felt nothing. Then he would administer the treatment that all burn patients come to know and loathe: manual debridement. Sloughing off the dead tissue felt like alcohol being poured into a wound, like red-hot pokers being jabbed into you, like your brains are being torn out through your hide—all of this centered on the patch of skin being scraped.

The first time I experienced this, I practically went crazy. I erupted into tears. Then I screamed and writhed. "Why are you doing this to me?" I howled as Mike rubbed the washcloth, called a fluff, back and forth across my wounds. "I've done nothing to you!" I reached up to his scrubs, clawed at them.

But debridement is the necessary evil of burn treatment. Dead tissue breeds infection, which is the most serious complication of a major burn injury. A burn wound is contaminated by bacteria, foreign tissue, and dead cells, and it's a farm for bacterial growth. Infection is responsible for 50 percent to 60 percent of deaths in burn patients. It's every caregiver's nightmare, and Mike wasn't having any of it.

"I'm sorry, buddy," he said. "I have to do this, and it'll benefit you down the road."

The road? My future? I didn't care. I wanted it to stop now. But it continued, every single morning. It was almost like being a child again and seeing my mom pull out the belt. I knew it was really for my own good, but that didn't make me like it any better.

And I began to hold it against Mike. Every morning in the tank I'd plead with him, "Why are you doing this to me?"

Every day the answer was the same: "You'll see. Someday you'll see what a difference this makes."

After my treatment, I was left alone to air-dry back in my room. No more pressure on my skin to cause more pain. I'd lie in the shower bed, the radio playing softly through the ceiling speakers. I'd listen to the words of each song—what else did I have to do?—and try to figure out if the singer was speaking to me. Christina Aguilera sang "You are beautiful," which only made me cry. I cried for the young man I had been and the person I was now. Even though I hadn't yet seen my burned face or body, I knew that I probably wasn't beautiful anymore. And that hurt almost as much as the physical pain.

After the tank, Dr. Barillo would come in to evaluate my wounds before they were dressed again and my skin lubricated with an anti-microbial cream to help prevent infection. Then I'd get some time to catch my breath, maybe have a nap before morning rehab.

In the early stages of my recovery, ICU rehab might be as "simple" as sitting in the "pink Cadillac"—the chair the staff used to help patients sit up and learn to breathe properly. I don't know why they call it a Cadillac, because it sure isn't comfortable like a fancy car; it's more like a torture contraption.

Then Mike would serve me my lunch while I visited with my mom. The afternoon activities included a reappearance by the rehab staff. Sometimes the occupational therapist would get me up to walk, she on one side and my mom on the other, helping me take those halting steps. Then I'd be returned to my bed and prepared for evening wound care. Dinner would come and go, visiting hours (and my mom's time at my side) would end, and Mike would say good night.

It went like that until one beautiful, bright Texas morning when I greeted Mike with a request. I'd had enough of the pain. I wanted to know what was causing it, why it hurt so badly when Mike cleaned my skin.

"I want to see my face and body."

Mike kept moving as if he hadn't heard me. He checked my chart, chatting about the usual stuff, news bits he'd heard on the radio, sports. The San Antonio Spurs had a good chance of winning the championship, he told me.

I repeated my request. He looked up from my chart. "Not now, man. You have plenty of time and many more surgeries. It's best to wait a while."

"Yes, now," I said. "I might as well see what I have to live with."

Mike stopped, thought for a second. "Okay,"

he said. "Give me a minute to get things set."

He reached for the pink Cadillac and rolled it to the window. He slid over the dining tray and opened the mirror compartment. He lifted me from the bed with the help of a therapist and settled me down into the seat. Somewhere below me, outside and in the distance, was Interstate 35, the cars moving along like Hot Wheels toward downtown.

"Whenever you're ready," Mike said, and moved away.

I took a deep breath, willing myself to turn my head toward the mirror. Still, it took many minutes to look, and when I finally did, the shock was physical.

I had seen someone like me once. I was with some buddies at a Mexican restaurant in Dalton when I spied a man who was dining with a couple of other people. His face was shriveled, mottled with ginger-colored spots and stringy scar tissue, his nostrils and eyes misshapen. His jaw swung at an odd angle. I'd never seen such a sight, and I tried to pull my gaze away. But I was curious, so finally I approached him.

"Sir, can I ask what happened to you?" I asked.

He looked at me, this cocky teenager who was busting in on his evening, with a kind expression. There had been a house fire, he said, and he'd gotten caught inside. We spoke for a minute or two.

"Sir, thank you for taking the time to explain what happened to you."

I returned to my friends, shaking my head and muttering, "There's no way I could ever go through that."

And now I was that guy.

Questions flooded my brain. Why did this happen to me? How can I live like this? Why was my life spared if I have to live this way? What girl will like me with looks like this? How could I reach any of my goals? Now I would never be a pro football player, and I wouldn't be able to be a good soldier, either. I couldn't feed myself with these clawlike hands. I couldn't even go to the bathroom in private. Would I always have to depend on my mother?

That night, I lay alone in the dark with the worst kind of insomnia, a mixture of sorrow and agony, wide-awake nightmares throwing me back into the explosion again and again, feeling the flames melt my flesh.

I woke, shaky and clammy, to find the night housekeeper cleaning my room. She was a familiar presence by then, although I had no idea what she looked like because she was wearing the same protective gear as everyone else who came into my room. She was just another set of eyes peeking out behind a mask. But I was comforted by the way she hummed softly as she worked. The tune sounded like a hymn, or maybe a lullaby. I closed my eyes and listened, and then I whispered, "Hello?" I hadn't initiated a conversation with anyone since I'd looked into the mirror that morning.

The woman apologized for disturbing me, but I wanted to talk. I asked her about her day and what other floors she cleaned.

Then another question tumbled from my mouth, out of nowhere.

"Has life been fair to you?" I asked her. I confided that I was in a bad place. "I think I would've been better off dying," I said.

She stopped her work, leaned over me. "You'll be fine." I could see the outline of her mouth beneath the sterile mask. "Everything is going to be all right."

"But why did this happen to me?" I asked her.

"I don't know," she said. "One day you'll find out."

I had told my mom I loved her nearly every day of my life. But I stopped telling her that after I saw my face. Instead, I'd shout at her: "Why? Why? Why?"

I didn't know who to blame, so I blamed everybody. In one instant, I'd morphed from a personable, cooperative patient to a mean, despondent shell. I grieved. I only spoke when spoken to; ate when fed. I wanted to torture everyone. *Who the hell cares,* I thought. I blocked everyone out. My mom felt sorry for Mike, having to put up with the nasty me all day long. As bad as those days were for me, they were nearly as bad for her. My care team called in reinforcements: a psychiatrist, a social worker, an occupational therapist, the hospital chaplain. Bonnie Jackson, the charge nurse, came in to flush me out.

"Nope, I'm not feeling it," I told her. "I don't want to be bothered."

She tried her usual burn patient logic on me: "You're so much more fortunate than so many others," she reminded me. "You're still the same person you were before you were injured. You can't afford to have that attitude. You've got to get up out of that bed."

But nothing stuck. I'd sit in that pink Cadillac every day hanging my head, eyes downcast or closed. I didn't want to look at anyone or answer anyone. I didn't tell anyone I wanted to die, but I did.

My mom was distraught. She didn't know how to help me; if the professionals couldn't rescue me, then who could? I'm just his mom, she thought. She didn't know what to say to me.

She went to the hospital chapel and prayed. Kneeling in a pew, she said: "Please, God, help me. Put special words in my mouth. Let me say your words and make him understand."

Emerging from the chapel, she heard the elevator ding. She got in and there was Mike.

He was red and hot. He shook his head at my mom.

"He isn't ready to listen," he told her.

My mom came to my room and went straight over to where I was sitting in the pink Cadillac.

"Hi, baby," she said. "How are you?"

No answer.

She got on her knees and put her arms on my legs. She put her face right under mine, so I'd have to lift my face. "Son, what's wrong?" she asked. She knew what was wrong, obviously, but she wanted to get me talking.

"My whole damn face has been burned!" I screamed. "Why are you asking me what's wrong?" I was crying.

She winced, fighting back her own tears. "Yeah, baby, and so is your body," she said. "Why do you only worry about your face and not your body? The problem is girls, right?"

I brought my eyes to hers. I nodded. "Yes, Mom."

She exhaled. "Listen, Jose Rene Martinez. If somebody is going to be in your life, it will be because of what you are inside," she said, pointing to my heart. "Not for what you are outside. If a girl or a mother or a friend wants to be by your side, it's for what you are on the inside. Many people are beautiful on the outside, but only God knows what their spirit looks like, because they carry that inside."

Her words somehow penetrated my brain. My

171

mind traveled back to high school and all the friends I'd had then. I wondered who'd liked me for what I'd been on the outside with no regard for the inside. Her words kindled a challenge in me: Now I'd find out who liked me for me. Really, it made sense.

"That's true, Mom," I told her. "I love you." My tears came again. We looked at each other and smiled.

As I was reconciling myself with my new face, I was still enveloped in loneliness, a feeling of isolation, like a speck of dust flicked off a world that was spinning along without me. At night I stared at the glass of the window, my vision blurred by tears. Each spring the city rolled out the welcome mat for the San Antonio Fiesta and thousands of visitors flooded in to enjoy live music, art, ceremonies, and events. Although I couldn't see out, I knew people were there, laughing, strolling down the River Walk, listening to the mariachis, munching their chips and salsa, floating on barges down the San Antonio River after their visit to the Alamo.

"Mike, tell me about it. What food is San Antonio known for? What do people do at Fiesta? Does it stay open late?"

I could hear the festivities—at least I thought I could—and the brilliant lights glittered through my window. I brooded about these unknown, unnamed people out there. Why were they able to have so much fun while I was up here in this hospital room, burned beyond recognition?

"One day," he said, "you'll get out of here and see Fiesta for yourself. Great food and music. Maybe by that time you can enjoy a margarita."

I wondered: *Will that ever happen?*

CHAPTER TEN

Burn Paradise

I had a long road ahead of me before I could seriously think about parties and cocktails. For now, I set my sights on something much more local: getting transferred from the ICU to 4E, the step-down wing of the burn unit.

I'd been hearing people talk about that place like it was burn paradise. Although it was just down the hall, it seemed a world away. The nurses told me that once I made it over there, the care wouldn't be as intense. I'd have a phone line in my room, so friends could call me. I'd have a TV right by my bed and be able to watch whatever, whenever. I already planned to have the hospital chow hall on speed dial.

The best part, though, was that I'd be able to get out of my room and walk around the ward. No matter how much pain you're in, no matter how much you worry about permanent disabilities or disfigurement, being left to stare at the same four walls day in, day out, week in, week out—that was the worst torture of all.

The dangling carrot of even that limited freedom

turned into a daily question: "Is today the day?"

"Not yet, J.R. Soon."

And then, forty-one days after I'd arrived in ICU, the time finally arrived. Hallelujah.

I could never have imagined how the sight of an orderly steering a wheelchair toward me would fill me with such profound joy. I said my goodbyes to the ICU staff. Even though I'd blamed Nurse Mike for all the physical pain I'd felt in debridement and for the psychic pain of seeing my face for the first time (although I knew neither was his fault), I was going to miss him.

Once I arrived in my new room I got to my feet and walked around, testing out everything. I checked out the bathroom, picked up the phone to hear the dial tone. My first order of business was to call the kitchen and order a Gatorade and a PBJ sandwich, my favorite hospital meal.

That said, while Unit 4E was better than ICU, it wasn't any nirvana. For starters, I contracted some kind of a bug, so I wasn't permitted to leave my room. The best I could do was stand inside the door, toeing an invisible line, calling out to the hallway traffic like I was some kind of Walmart greeter. The nurses' station was right in front of my room, so I entertained myself for hours watch-ing the nurses come and go and visitors entering and exiting the ward. Other patients strolled the corridors, getting their exercise or heading to the gym for therapy.

Over time, other patients' families became familiar to me, and we'd say hello to one another.

"Hi, J.R. How are you doing today, baby?" someone would ask.

"Great," I'd reply, trying to keep them lingering with me as long as possible.

My mom spent about twelve hours a day, every day, at my bedside. One of our daily pastimes was looking at the mail that came into the hospital for me. I received letters from the guys in my unit back in Iraq, including from my lieutenant, the one who'd smoked me for dissing the Army brotherhood. I also got letters from people back in Hope and Dalton. Even schoolkids wrote to me. Those cards and letters made me so happy. They reconnected me to life outside the hospital walls. My mom and I read them together and shared the memories that some of them evoked.

One afternoon I told my mom about a bizarre dream I'd had: I was at a NASCAR driver's house for a barbecue, but I was inside, sitting on the couch in the living room, isolated, unable to join the other guests outside. I spotted a snake sliding across the rug toward me. I looked around wildly to see if anyone would rescue me. In an instant, the snake flung itself toward me, right into my mouth. I wrapped my hands around its slick body and yanked. My mother rushed to my side, but instead of helping me, she just stood there and cried. The other guests crowded into the house.

As a group, they pushed the snake deeper into my mouth as I gagged.

After I told my mom this story, the two of us analyzed it and figured out that it was about the doctors treating me. Anyway, in that room we talked about pretty much everything under the sun—my recovery, the pain I was still experiencing, my mom's current living situation, whether her bill payments were up-to-date, and how much money she had in her bank account. Her absence from work was hitting her hard in the pocketbook, so we spent time figuring out how to rob Peter to pay Paul. I'd nap, we'd watch TV, and every evening we'd watch the Spanish soaps.

At night, the entertainment options dried up. My mom went back to her room across the street from the hospital, the therapy and technician appointments ceased, and the halls got real quiet. The night nurses came in for their shifts, talking in low voices so as not to disturb sleeping patients. Lucky bastards.

For me, sleep was as elusive as the parking lot outside. I had too much energy and there was nothing to do locked up in my room all day. I made myself into a pest, calling out to the staff, straining to get their attention. I was like a pound puppy, trying to get people to notice me.

"Watch out, I'm coming out!" I'd threaten, waving a foot over the threshold.

"Martinez! Knock it off and go to sleep!"

My food and liquid intake was carefully monitored, so if I'd used up my Gatorade allotment for the day, I'd try to cajole one of the young male staff to duck into the supply room and bring me out a drink.

"Hey, man, just do it this once," I'd plead. "Get me an orange one!"

Sometimes they'd do it, just to shut me up.

I underwent seven of my thirty-three operations during my thirty-two days in 4E. I'd already endured many rounds of excision and grafting, a primary technique that calls for the dead tissue to be excised, or cut off, from the burn, and transplanting healthy skin onto damaged areas. Whenever possible, they harvest the patient's own skin for use, a technique called autograft. Prior to the procedure, a technician uses a special device to slice healthy tissue from the patient's donor site. The surgeon grafts the healthy skin onto the clean wound bed, stapling it securely and blanketing it with medication and protective dressings. The goal is to cover all the wounds so that the patient doesn't develop an infection.

If doctors have to use skin from a tissue bank, they try to match the skin tone to the patient's. (Allograft, or cadaver skin from tissue banks, normally only serves as a temporary dressing. When the patient's immune system begins to function again, the skin-bank skin is rejected by the body as foreign.) For an area where there's lots of hair growing, for example, doctors will choose a section of donor skin where hair would ordinarily grow. Tissue is used from all parts of the body. They sometimes even use scrotal tissue on the eyelids because the tissue at that location is thinner. Small mercy, I was spared that particular procedure.

Like most burn patients, I welcomed the corrections, but sometimes they felt like setbacks. Just as I was starting to feel more human, I would be in for more pain and discomfort. If they harvested skin from one leg to graft it on the other, both legs would come out hurting. If the skin was coming from the bank, there was an additional blood draw, called a "type and cross," to deter-mine compatibility between patient serum and donor red blood cells. Then the patient is desig-nated NPO, meaning nothing by mouth, for eight hours prior to surgery. If an emergency crops up and surgery is pushed back, a patient could end up NPO for twelve hours or more. Calorie intake is critical in burn patients, so it can be an impediment when someone doesn't receive the proper nutrition, even for eight hours. Antibiotics usually are ordered, so the patient has to have an IV hooked up while the drugs infuse. And depending on what part of the body is being worked on, patients may temporarily lose the mobility they had worked so hard to regain.

So yeah, I got irritable about it, even though I knew that each surgery would get me closer to feeling and looking better.

Dr. Barillo surprised me once in a way that was almost funny. He explained one surgery to work on my eye and my hand, adding that he'd do an "ear trim" as well. I assumed that my left ear hadn't been severely burned, but nearly every morning I'd find tiny pieces of skin that had flaked from my ear onto my pillow. Ear burns usually are deep because the skin is so thin. They also are prone to a special type of infection called chondritis, because the cartilage of the ear does not have its own blood supply and must depend on the skin. Ears are difficult to reconstruct, so surgeons try to leave as much tissue in place as possible. In my case, it became obvious that the external ear wasn't alive, so Dr. Barillo would try to trim back to living tissue. Rather than do this at my bedside a little every day, he elected to trim the dead stuff off under anesthesia along with these other operations. Unfortunately, by the time he got to healthy tissue, all of the external ear was gone.

When I woke up from the surgery, I looked in the mirror. My left ear was missing. "They said this was a trim, but it was an amputation!" I shouted to my mom. All we could do was look at each other and laugh. While this had been the clear plan to the surgical team, I guess I hadn't understood it well beforehand.

In both the ICU and 4E, I received visitors other than my mom. My godmother, Alejandra, came, bringing her daughters Katrina and Lisa. Claudia, a former girlfriend from Hope, came several times on the Greyhound bus. That was great, because I felt like I got points with the nurses for having pretty girls in my room.

And in mid-May I had a few extra-special visitors: Lieutenant General Robert T. Clark and his aides came to my room to award me the Purple Heart, a combat decoration for those who've been wounded while serving in the military.

It's an honor to receive this decoration, but in my own heart I didn't believe I'd really earned it. The Purple Heart is presented to people who've done badass stuff. Prior to enlisting I'd spoken to a couple of Vietnam vets whose bravery and courage truly seemed to justify receiving it. They'd been in firefights, seen their friends pass away, killed enemy combatants. I'd done none of this. I'd just been driving along and had happened to hit a bomb.

I spent my twentieth birthday on June 14 with my mom and Celestino, who'd driven in from Dalton to join us. It was the first time I was permitted to leave the grounds of Fort Sam Houston and take a look at the city of San Antonio. I was excited to see what the place was all about.

A few days earlier my mom and I had gone

on a shopping spree to the base exchange. The Army had allotted me some money to buy clothing so that I could have something to wear outside the hospital. I bought two pairs of basketball shorts—white and blue—that would slide over my hips, a couple of T-shirts, a pair of shoes, and underwear. Athletic shorts were the easiest for me, as I couldn't handle buttons and they're easy to pull on and off.

My mom helped me dress for our outing. She pulled a shirt over my head, being careful not to rub my ears with the fabric. She tugged on my white shorts with the red piping, a red baseball cap, and my shoes.

I could hardly contain myself as we walked down the halls of 4E to the elevator. Celestino was waiting out front in my Maxima. My mom climbed into the back, I settled into the passenger seat, and we were off. The 25 mph speed limit on the base felt like we were crawling by inches.

A Mexican restaurant on the River Walk was our first stop for an early dinner. The River Walk is a five-mile public park along the banks of the San Antonio River in the city's downtown. Lined with shops and restaurants and museums and theaters, it's touted as the "biggest tourist attraction in Texas."

Though I was happy to be outside the gates of the base, the afternoon's late heat weighed me down. I wore compression garments underneath my clothing. Applying constant pressure to my skin, the garments help prevent hard, irregular scar tissue from forming and ease the ever-present itch of the burned areas. I had to wear these garments twenty-three hours a day. Under the Texas sun, they felt like armor.

As we waited outside for our table, I got the first taste of being an object of fascination. It wasn't just my wrinkled bright red skin. The doctors had sewn a yellow bolster into my eyelid to help remold it; the effect was especially jarring.

We were seated at a table and ordered off the menu. My mom summoned mariachis to play for my birthday, which was embarrassing.

After we finished eating, we strolled along the River Walk. I willed myself to get used to the stares. The adults tried to be sly about it—most were not unkind—and I couldn't blame little kids for gawking.

Those few hours out showed me what the road ahead might look like for me. I could see it was going to be difficult. I'd figured that people would stare at me, and they certainly did. Knowing I looked different was hard enough. Now the reaction of other people would remind me every time I stepped out into the world. The worst was back at the restaurant when I'd noticed a couple of cute girls look at me and quickly turn away. I wondered how the girls back home in Dalton would treat me.

Home. I'd been thinking about it practically since I'd woken up in San Antonio. And now it was time. My care team decided that I was well enough to enjoy a month of convalescent leave in Dalton.

My mom asked me if I wanted her to invite people over to say hello when I got back, or if I wanted to take it easy for a few days after my return and then gradually see my friends. I thought this was going to be the true test of how people were going to accept me. I certainly wasn't shy about seeing my friends. My mom said that she would have to go back a few days earlier than me so she could get everything ready at the house. My mind interpreted that as "surprise party!" and I envisioned people gathering at my house, eating good food, and visiting with old friends, nothing else. I didn't let on to my mom that I suspected a thing.

While we were talking, my social worker came to my room. She also asked me if I was open to people seeing me as soon as I got home. I said yes. She mentioned that Dalton's local media had expressed interest to the hospital about my return to Georgia, and she wondered whether it would be too much for me at once. Nope, I told her, I can do it. I want to do it.

Just then Norma Guerra passed by. Norma was the chief of public affairs for BAMC. The social worker motioned her over and told her that we were discussing the best course for me on leave. Norma reiterated that media had found out that I would be going home. My doctors had mentioned to her that it might be best for me to stay on the down-low because too much attention could be overwhelming.

"I don't suggest you go there and on the first day have parades and stuff," Norma said. "You need to be convalescing. How about you wait a week or so and we can schedule a press conference for you?"

"I'll be fine," I told her. "I don't care if there are a lot of people there at the beginning."

I knew how much everyone's prayers and good wishes meant to my recovery and rather than being overwhelmed, I was excited to be surrounded by my supporters in person, to feel their energy and love. Given my physical state, Norma and my social worker arranged for an escort to help me on the flight from San Antonio to Chattanooga, with a plane change in Chicago. My hands were still pretty useless—my fingers were fused together by scar tissue that had formed at the second knuckle. I could barely close my hands enough to grip my boarding pass. I couldn't reach into my pocket to pull out money, either. I definitely needed help. The escort would assist me with everything from carrying my luggage to paying cashiers for my food and drinks to dealing with my tickets.

We were scheduled to arrive in Chattanooga at around four in the afternoon, but in Chicago we got word that our connecting flight would be delayed, pushing our arrival time back to 10 p.m. *Damn,* I thought. *I won't be able to see anyone until tomorrow.* Honestly, I wasn't looking forward to seeing anyone in particular. I just wanted to be home.

I was especially eager to see how I'd be received.

A man sitting next to me at the airport asked if my name was J. R. Martinez. "I'm Coach McClurg's son," he said, remembering me from the football team. I hadn't expected anyone from Dalton, Georgia, to be sitting next to me in the Chicago airport. We spent a couple of hours talking, mostly about my injury but also about Coach McClurg and Catamount football. The unexpected distraction was a godsend. By the time we boarded, I had an extra spring to my step.

I dozed during the short flight, and when the plane landed my escort and I stayed seated while everyone else deplaned. Many of my wounds were still open, and I was embarrassed to see that I had bled slightly on the seatback cover. Once the other passengers were gone, my escort led me off the plane.

I was surprised to see all my plane mates lining each side of the jetway. As I walked through, they clapped for me.

"How do they know?" I asked my escort. It felt so good.

Coach McClurg was the first person I saw when I peered past security. I walked right into his arms and didn't hold back my tears.

"You're home, J.R.," he said into my ear.

A couple of local news crews shone their lights on my face to highlight the open wounds and scars. They shot my reaction as I craned my neck to look for my mom and embraced the dozen friends who had been waiting for me. No one seemed to care that they were hugging this charred body. When my mom appeared, we greeted each other as if it had been years instead of a few days. I jumped into the passenger seat of Gabriel's car, which was outfitted with bells and whistles. I had trouble buckling my seat belt, another reminder of my new disabilities. Gabriel noticed I was struggling and leaned over to help me click in the buckle. We merged onto I-75 with the engine roaring and the bass thumping my favorite songs—hip-hop, Spanish rap, reggaeton. A couple of friends in the backseat asked me about my time in Iraq, and I had to shout over the noise.

At exit 333, Walnut Avenue in Dalton, Gabriel stopped for a red light.

"Get out here," he told me.

"Why, man?" We weren't anywhere near my mom's apartment. We were on the off-ramp. My door was yanked open from the outside.

"Come on, boy." It was my friend Aaron, a big jokester. "Get out of the car."

This was obviously one of his pranks, I thought, climbing out.

And then a police car pulled up beside me, lights flashing. *Oh my God,* I thought. *Here I survived a bomb blast in Iraq and now I get arrested the minute I get back home, all because of my bonehead friends.*

A black convertible rolled up behind the flashing lights. It was a replica of a 1932 Mercedes- Benz, a sweet piece of machinery. My jaw dropped when the driver stuck out his head.

"Well, hey, J.R. Why don't you hop in the backseat and let's go for a ride?" It was the husband of Dalton High's principal back when I was a senior.

I looked at Aaron. "Get in," he urged. He helped me into the car and settled me on the top of the rear seat. He sat next to me, one arm around my waist to keep me in place. "Hold on, boy," he said, "we're gonna take you for a ride."

The driver hit the gas, turning onto Walnut Avenue, the police car leading the way. My mouth fell open in shock.

As we approached the McDonald's on the right-hand side, I saw people standing on the shoulder of the road. They waved at me, yelling, "We love you!" As we slowly drove down Walnut, we passed the Applebee's restaurant. I read the marquee: "Welcome Home J.R. You Are Our Hero and We Love You."

I looked at Aaron. "This is crazy, man!" I told him.

"The best is yet to come," he replied, pointing over to my left at the Kmart.

Our Mercedes pulled into the parking lot, where a huge crowd waited next to a trailer stage. I saw Coach McClurg, my former teammates, high school friends, and old girlfriends—as well as people I didn't even know. Aaron helped me out of the car and onto the stage. I'd never felt such surprise and shock. I was especially amazed that all these people had come together for me at this hour of the night.

My former teammates took turns speaking, and then my coach spoke. They talked about how strong I was, what an asset I'd been to the team. Coach McClurg told the now familiar story about how I'd moved to Dalton and gotten myself a place on the football team.

As he presented me with the key to the city—a gold-plated old key with teeth—camera flashes sparkled in the darkness. Someone asked me to speak. I don't recall what I said, how I sounded, or how long I talked, but I remember looking out into the audience and making eye contact with all these people I knew. I felt enveloped in love and acceptance. Once I was finished I carefully got down from the stage and made my way through the crowd, saying hello and hugging people.

My disfigurements had ceased to exist from the first moment I'd hopped into Gabriel's car. The love I felt from these people erased the pain, worries, and thoughts of my scarred existence.

I worked my way to a friend's car, and he took me to my mom's place, which was all decorated in red, white, and blue. People spilled out the front door. I felt like their hero.

Is this the way it's going to be from here on out? I wondered. *Would there always be this many people to support me?*

It was summer already and those friends who'd gone to college had arrived back in Dalton. Those who hadn't left had moved on to jobs in town. During that month back home I felt like I'd never left. My friends would come over to the apartment, we'd go cruising, and we would walk through the mall looking in store windows, hanging out, checking out the girls. Sure, people stared at me, but my friends said, "Forget those people. They don't know you."

I felt as if I were doing everything a twenty-year-old should be doing, and my life was going to be just fine. One of my friends had a cookout, inviting all the seniors from the football team as well as a few girls. It took me back to when I was in high school and made me feel normal.

That is, until the burgers were served.

My injury made it impossible for me to eat normally. One side of my mouth was burned, and the scar tissue prevented me from opening it more than a little bit. I sat in this group of my friends, staring down at my plate, stymied by the challenge a simple hamburger presented.

I picked it up awkwardly with both hands and put it to my mouth, but I was only able to take a small bite out of the burger. The rest fell out of my clawed hands onto the plate. I didn't know who saw me, but I was totally embarrassed.

Aaron came to my rescue. He reached over and said, as only Aaron could, "You crazy Mexican. You can't eat a burger? I'll help you out, buddy," and he cut my burger into pieces small enough to fit into my mouth.

I was incredibly grateful that he took something that was excruciating for me and made it a matter we could laugh about. I've never forgotten this. And yet it was just one of the many, many demonstrations of love I experienced during my month at home.

As the time neared for my trip back to San Antonio, I started to get nervous. I wasn't going to have anyone with me to help this time. My mother was anxious about my solo flight as well. I repeatedly assured her that I'd be fine, although I didn't really feel that way. I'd had thirty days to prepare, though, and I did the best I could by stretching. But my fingers were still stiff and stuck in a position as if I were grabbing something. It was difficult to grasp things inside my pockets, feed myself, hold a drink, use the bathroom, and button my pants up—and almost everything else we use our hands for.

When the day arrived, my mom and I drove to the airport. She helped me get my boarding pass, but once I was in the security line the help was gone. However, my mother and I had planned for this and were very strategic when it came to choosing my wardrobe for this flight: I wore clothing and shoes that were easy to get in and out of, which was important in this post-shoe-bomber world that required all footwear to go through the scanner.

Once I was through security, I picked up my belongings and turned around to wave at my mother, who was standing along the security wall. She smiled and waved back.

As I headed off toward my departure gate, I felt a great sense of accomplishment. But just to be safe, I kept my boarding pass in my hand until it was time to give it to the gate agent.

Between flights in Chicago, I got thirsty. *I can do this,* I thought. I went into a store, grabbed a Dr Pepper from the refrigerator, and walked over to the cashier. There were a few people in front of me in line. I tried to look casual, but I was dreading the moment when I would have to pull money from my pocket and pay. How would I look trying to get it out? If I dropped change on the floor, would I be able to pick it up? Would people laugh at me?

Finally, it was my turn at the register. The cashier stared at my open wounds and disfigurement before correcting herself and looking down at her machine. She rang up my drink and told me the total. I took a breath and nodded my head to her. With one hand I clasped the outside of my pocket and pulled it open enough so my other hand could reach in and grab the money. I slid the bills along the lining of my pants. As they got to the top of the pocket, I pulled them out and gave them to her. I was ecstatic.

And then, to my horror, I realized the cashier was trying to give me change! What was I supposed to do? I figured my options were: walk away to avoid humiliation, or face my fear and give it a try. I knew she would put the coins in my hand. The problem was I couldn't make a fist or grasp things. I also couldn't turn my palms upward— what the rehab docs called supinate. At this point in my recovery, I couldn't lift flat objects off any flat surface, either. To top it off, my hands were weak and numb.

I've come to believe that when you overthink something, you're ultimately inviting it to happen. This can be good or bad. In this case, bad: I kept visualizing myself dropping the change and sure enough I did. "Damn!" I said. A man behind me stepped in to help, picking up the coins and dropping them into my hand. I met his eyes and thanked him.

I boarded my flight as soon as my zone was called so I wouldn't hold up anyone who was getting on behind me, but I couldn't avoid the stares of the passengers waiting in the aisle for me to get to my seat.

A soldier who worked at BAMC met me at the airport in San Antonio. He helped me with my luggage and drove me back to the base.

I was assigned a room in the guesthouse, the inn across the street from the hospital where my mother had stayed. The following day I had to report to my doctor to go over the plans for the upcoming months. He told me that my job for the foreseeable future was to focus on my recovery and nothing else.

For the remainder of the summer I spent hours in therapy, meeting with plastic surgeons to discuss the next steps in my reconstruction, and watching daytime television. In August, although I was tentative about this procedure, surgeons implanted a tissue expander into my chest to stimulate my body to grow additional skin to use on my burned areas. The expander is a water-filled balloon that is placed under the skin and gradually inflated. As the balloon increases in size, the skin covering accommodates it by growing new cells.

About a month later, in September, I started to

feel feverish, with pain in the chest area around the expander. The doctors removed it immediately. I should have been relieved, but it meant I'd have to start the uncomfortable process all over again.

Some of the other surgeries I underwent in the months after the explosion were bizarre in their own right. I had developed something called heterotopic ossification in my right forearm. This strange condition happens when bone tissue forms outside the skeleton. It's predominantly seen in patients who experience multiple traumatic injuries at one time or burn injuries. I'd had both. The way to fix it is to go in and cut it out.

When burned skin begins to heal, whether on its own or with a graft, it tends to become tighter than it was originally. It's what the medical professionals call contracture, and it has the effect of pulling on surrounding tissue. To correct it, they do a "contracture release" to reduce that tightness. I had this done on my upper and lower eyelids so that I could close my eyes properly.

Because my hands were so badly burned, doctors had implanted a Kirschner wire, or K-wire, which is a stainless steel pin used to immobilize a joint. In my case, they put it in the first joints of my fingers to keep my fingers fixed in full extension to reduce the contracture as my skin healed.

I'd also suffered a very bad fracture in my right

ulna, or elbow bone, so the doctors had installed a plate with screws to hold it together. I was starting to see the parallels between modern medicine and carpentry.

But as unpleasant as the therapies and surgeries and exercises were, the boredom was what really got to me. Young men aren't designed to sit around all day. The only people I knew were the hospital staff and the people who worked at the guesthouse where I was staying. I grew bored with the hours of TV—especially the soaps that seemed to saturate the scheduling. I desperately needed to do something productive outside of the daily appointments, eating, and watching TV. All the days blended together.

The front-desk receptionist at 4E was a gregarious Puerto Rican woman named Christina. I found myself talking to her a lot because she was fun. Her husband was a drill sergeant in the Air Force. One weekend she and her husband picked me up from the hospital and took me to their house for dinner. While Christina cooked, her husband and I sat and chatted about all sorts of things. We ate and fell into a semi-coma. Then we talked about how much we'd eaten and how we should have saved ourselves from discomfort by refusing that last bite. Toward the end of the evening, they took me back to my lonely and boring hotel room.

The following Monday morning, I was back at

the 4E nurses' station, looking for distraction. And then someone asked me to run a few errands in the hospital. From that point on, I was the guy who ran errands. I loved it because it made me feel important and gave me something to do with my time.

It was also in September that I had my first romantic encounter with a girl since my accident. (Well, technically it wasn't my first—I'd hung out in Dalton with my old girlfriend Daniela, but that didn't really count because I figured she had probably just been stuck on the old J.R. anyway.) This girl's name was Amelia. She was the eighteen-year-old daughter of a woman who worked at the guesthouse, and we'd met when she'd visited her mom at work. We hung out a couple of times and I enjoyed her company.

One afternoon, her mom dropped her off at my room for a visit. We snuggled up on the couch to watch a movie, and we started to make out. One thing led to another, and she gently tried to tug off my shirt. I resisted. What would she think about these scars?

"Don't worry about it," she said in my ear, and off came the shirt. She touched the scars on my arm and then on my chest and stomach. I anxiously watched her face for signs that she was turned off, but I saw none.

This was another major turning point for me in my recovery.

● ● ●

I had another turning point of a completely different sort that month. One day after I'd run the usual few errands around the hospital and had my therapy appointment, one of the nurses asked me a question: "Would you be willing to talk with a patient I'm treating?"

I didn't understand what she wanted me to do.

"He isn't doing very well and is really down on himself," she said. "His injuries aren't that severe, and I've been trying to explain to him that it will get better, but he's not responding."

I thought about it for a while, wondering what, if anything, I could bring to this person. "Sure," I said. "I'll do it."

Still, the idea of visiting a complete stranger made me nervous. What if I said something wrong that negatively impacted him? Swallowing my unease, I made my way to his room. I put on the sterile garb just outside his door, the same head-to-toe outfit visitors had worn in my room during those first weeks. I took a breath and walked in.

The room was dark. The blinds were closed, and the lights were off. And it was completely silent. It was as if the patient had already exited this world.

I approached his bed and introduced myself as a burn patient. And then I just started talking. I told him about my injury and how I'd made it to San Antonio. I told him about my weeks in the

ICU and the feelings of despair I'd had there. I told him about my reaction when I first saw my face.

Since I couldn't see him, I asked him if his face was burned.

"Yeah," he said, "but not a lot." He was mostly burned on his body—his limbs.

I used that as a stepping-stone. "Well, you got it made, man," I told him. "You'll be able to cover up your burns with long sleeves. My face is hard to cover." I wasn't trying to minimize his pain, but I wanted to emphasize the fact that even if you think your situation is severe, there's always going to be someone who's got it worse.

Case in point: About a month after I saw my face, I was looking out into the hallway of 4E. A young man hobbled by my door. His face was almost completely gone. I was stunned. I whirled around and told my mom: "I'll never complain again."

The young man I was visiting had "only" second-degree burns on his arm and face. "You're going to be fine," I told him. "Listen, I know your body has changed, too, but the truth is you're going to heal great. The pinkness will fade away in time, and your scars will heal if you pay attention to the advice the medical team here is giving you. I know this because I've already seen improve-ments in my own appearance."

He didn't say much, so I just kept yammering

away. After a while I switched direction, talking about the military, my life growing up, and girls. I told him about my recent visit home and how that trip had made me realize that my life had changed and I had to go with it.

"You and me, we're standing in one spot and watching the world move around us. If we don't want to get left behind, we have to move with it." For me, that meant I needed to make the best of it until I found a way to make sense of my new body.

We visited for about forty-five minutes that day.

"Can I bring you anything tomorrow?" I asked as I was leaving.

"I'll take a couple of magazines so I can read up on what's going on in the world," he said.

"I'm on it, man," I replied, and practically skipped to the door.

As I removed my sterile gear in the hallway, I looked back and saw that he'd turned on the lights above his bed and opened the curtain to his big picture window.

"Be sure to enjoy the view. You've been given a new set of eyes to see it from," I said.

I reached for the hand sanitizer, a big smile on my face. I felt great—empowered even.

When I reported back to the nurse who'd asked me to spend some time with this patient, she said, "See, J.R., I knew you could help him."

I walked straight out of the hospital and back to

my room in the guesthouse, grabbed the phone, and called my mom.

"Remember, Mom, how I asked you and everyone else why this had happened to us?"

Yes, she replied, she remembered.

"I think I have the answer to the question now. I think I was kept here to help other people with their own difficult experiences."

My mom let out a knowing giggle. "I think you're right, mijo."

We hung up and I went right back over to the hospital. I put in a request to speak to the head of the burn ward. I thought it was important to obtain clearance from the top.

"I want to help," I told him.

From then on, my daily routine had a new purpose. Every morning, I grabbed breakfast at the hospital and went straight to the fourth floor to eat. Then I'd head out to my morning therapy sessions. After lunch, I'd walk the halls, looking in on patients and asking the nurses who could benefit from a visit.

My mom told me about an older gentleman, David Jayne, whom she had met during those weeks when she was at my bedside in ICU. Jayne himself had been burned in an Army helicopter fire in 1959 and had spent more than three years recovering in BAMC before returning to duty and then embarking on a second career as an attorney. In 1994 he and his wife, Jane, cofounded the Texas Burn Survivor Society. Once a month, Mr. Jayne walked the halls of BAMC, speaking to burn patients.

The Jaynes also scheduled a monthly counseling session within the walls of BAMC to which they'd invite ambulatory patients and their families. My mother told me about one of the meetings she'd attended. She told me that Mr. Jayne's face was severely scarred from his burns, but that I needed to see him with my own eyes and hear his message with my own ears to really get it.

One night I was allowed to leave my 4E room, and it happened to be a night when the Jaynes were holding their support session. My mom and I attended the group meeting. I took my turn to speak about what had happened to me and the challenges I faced.

I had felt validated to be able to tell my story and look out at the circle of nodding heads. That experience showed me the power in sharing feelings. If I could go into patients' rooms and bring this experience to them, catching them early in their recovery, maybe I could reach people at the juncture of optimism and depression and help them choose hope.

The days flew by. At seven or eight in the evening, I'd begin my walk back to the guesthouse, first stopping by the chow hall in the hospital basement to grab dinner. I got to know many of the cashiers—I ate for free but they still had to tally up my selections—and enjoyed messing with them. I always headed straight for the heart-attack food—grilled-cheese sandwiches, buffalo wings, hamburgers, fries. I suppose that partially explains why I gained so much weight in the hospital. Once in a while I ran into a staff member I knew, and we'd eat together in the cafeteria, but most nights I took my mountains of food and a giant soda back to my room to eat in front of the TV.

My room was usually freezing cold from the air-conditioning, but that was good for me. The walk from the hospital often caused me to work up a major sweat. Sweat glands are destroyed with deep partial-thickness or full-thickness burns, and they're not restored once the skin heals. I would always have issues in controlling body temperature, and the Texas heat and humidity added to my discomfort.

My new undertaking of visiting patients around my own recovery proved to be exhausting. Every evening when I left the hospital and returned to my room, I felt like I'd put in a full day's work at the plant. But this new routine offered me a purpose and demanded a commitment.

I liked to get up close to patients, so I could look them in the eyes and they could see my wounds for themselves. Although my facial burns weren't the worst they could be, the fact remained that I wasn't able to hide them from the world. I had to display them every single day. I wanted to show these other patients the details of my scars, say to them, in essence, "I'm not afraid to show my face every day, and if I can do it with such visible wounds, you can, too."

"Listen," I'd say to them. "Yeah, we have it hard and it's tough, but it's who we are and it's our job to show the world that we're not different inside, even though we may look different on the outside."

We'd talk about the issues surrounding their daily recovery and anything else going on in their world. They'd asked me questions about my recovery. If they were due for a surgery, they'd ask me about my experience with that procedure. Since I'd had so many, I often was able to speak to them from true experience.

Visiting patients made me feel good, like I was giving something back. It also served as a great distraction from the grueling and repetitive nature of my day-to-day life in recovery.

And then I found another way to give back.

The BAMC public affairs staff asked me to sit for an interview with a local media outlet. The media were clamoring for feel-good stories about the war. The fact that I was visiting other wounded troops qualified me.

I'd only done a couple of very brief interviews before, and I laugh now to think of my responses to the reporter's questions: vague and monosyllabic answers, punctuated by lots of "ummmms" and "uhhhhhs."

By November, when the CBS newsmagazine *60 Minutes* came to town, I was more polished. Public affairs had prepped me for this one, giving me guidelines and talking points. I assured them that I wouldn't say anything inappropriate. My aim was to stay as positive as I could, and I think I hit the target.

When Pentagon correspondent David Martin asked me if I noticed people looking at my scars, I said, "Yes, it's happened a lot. I just say to myself, 'I know why I look like this, and you don't.' "

My face was still red, raw, and puffy, and my head was covered by a blue baseball cap. I'd already been through many surgeries, and I didn't know what the end result would be. But, I told Martin, "I've seen pictures of what things can turn out to be, and to me, it's amazing. I'm like, 'Wow, I can be back to what I used to be.' "

Just after the *60 Minutes* interview, and six months after my accident, the Army transferred me back to Fort Campbell. Regardless of my injuries I was still an active-duty soldier, so I was ordered to report to my unit to perform whatever chores I was assigned. The Army believed that the doctors at Blanchfield Army Community

Hospital could ably continue my care. They also arranged for me to visit the burn surgeons at Vanderbilt University Medical Center in nearby Nashville so they could perform any plastic surgeries I still needed.

My responsibilities at the unit usually consisted of answering phones and delivering paperwork. It annoyed me to take orders from people who'd never deployed. I had no one to hang out with because all my friends were still in Iraq. The base was basically deserted, and the few people remaining there were strangers. Every day was a huge bore. I couldn't wait to hit civilian soil at the end of each day, and luckily I was able to do just that.

My former sergeant, Chris Valdez—one of the soldiers who had pulled me from the burning Humvee—had a home outside the base. Although he was still overseas with our unit, he and his ex-wife, Hope, invited me to stay at their house with Hope and their young son while I was at Fort Campbell. I was grateful for the offer. Hope made home-cooked meals, I played hard with little Chris, and the three of us went out to eat and to the movies.

And I was able to go home to Dalton to spend Thanksgiving and Christmas with my mom.

In the new year, I made it over to Vanderbilt, but the doctors there ultimately decided they couldn't offer me the care I required. They suggested that it would be medically best for me to return to BAMC to continue treatment with the providers who'd cared for me from the beginning. As my friends in New York would say: Oy vey. I called my social worker at BAMC and told her; within weeks I had orders in hand back to BAMC.

Before I left to go back to San Antonio in February 2004, my unit returned home to Fort Campbell, nearly a year after we'd boarded the airliner east to Kuwait. It was a day I'd played over in my mind again and again, each time with a common theme: My buddies would all rush toward me with tears in their eyes. There would be lots of man-hugs and backslaps, followed by hours of beers and camaraderie.

That's not how it went.

Although I did hug a few of the guys, tears running down my face, I felt strangely disconnected. My close friends were happy to see me, but they were also greeting their wives and children, parents, girlfriends, and other friends. After a few words with each, I was left standing alone. I managed to feel, again, that I wasn't part of the brotherhood. I hadn't experienced what they'd been through over the last months, and none of them seemed very interested in the details of my recovery.

I told a group of guys that I'd been awarded the Purple Heart. "Why did you get that?" asked one guy who was a real ass even in the best of times. "Your Humvee didn't run over a mine. You were hit by friendly fire."

I knew that was bullshit, but it still stung that this "brother" would say such a thing to me.

"A Purple Heart doesn't matter," I said. "My story is about *what* happened to me and how I survived, not about *how* it happened to me."

I walked away from him, ready to get off base, away from these people.

Even one of my best friends, PJ, didn't really have time for me; his girlfriend from Nebraska had come to Fort Campbell to welcome him home. I understood—really, I did—but it still hurt.

PJ and his girlfriend drove me to the Nashville airport for my flight to San Antonio. Once I got through security to my gate and sat to collect my thoughts, I wondered why I'd even gone to the homecoming. It hadn't done anything for me to see the guys return, and it didn't do them any good to see me, either. I hadn't been with them long enough to build a strong bond, and as long as they didn't have to count me as a KIA, they moved on.

Back at BAMC, I noticed that other patients received visits from the guys they'd served with. No one visited me. After finally having been sold on the brotherhood, I felt that they had forgotten about me.

I never once took a step back to consider how the events of April 5, 2003, might also have changed the lives of those young soldiers. In fact, the soldiers who had been directly involved had been recognized for their bravery and sacrifice with Purple Hearts and Army Commendations; O'Shea had received the Soldier's Medal. In those years after the explosion, though, it was only about me, and it would take a long time for me to see things differently.

CHAPTER ELEVEN

A Long Road Home

It was the spring of 2004. I strolled through the sliding-glass doors of the hospital like I always did, but it was obvious this wasn't a regular day. You'd have thought the president was paying a visit. The lobby was closed off to regular visitors and patients, and military guards were stationed throughout for security.

"I'm one of the soldiers Oprah's going to interview," I told the sentries at the door, and they parted so I could go to the elevator, which I took to the fourth floor.

I'd been chosen as one of five troops she'd speak to, and I was very excited about the opportunity. A few nights prior to the event, I lay awake all night channel surfing for her show. I wanted to understand her interview style so our meeting would be powerful and I'd make a good impres-sion on her.

The star hadn't yet arrived, so the other soldiers —all amputees—and I hung around waiting. And waiting. And waiting. I was starving, but I couldn't leave the floor to grab a bite because Oprah might show up while I was gone. I didn't want to keep her waiting, did I?

Finally she turned up. She greeted us brusquely.

"I can't believe I'm meeting you!" I said.

She smiled and turned to her producers. "Here we go," she said.

Then it was back to business as usual. My mother had visited but gone back to Dalton, and I found myself sitting in my room night after night with only the television screen for company. I played Halo on Xbox, using a headset to compete online with players around the world. I'd watch sports, mostly basketball—I loved the Sacramento Kings with Mike Bibby, Chris Webber, Peja Stojakovic, and Vlade Divac.

The boring routine was broken up again one day when the owner of the Dallas Mavericks invited eight troops from BAMC to fly on his private jet to see his team play, and I was one of the lucky ones. I got to meet Steve Nash and Dirk Nowitzki, the star players, as well as Tony Delk.

I'd checked back into my room at the guest-house some weeks earlier after returning from Fort Campbell. I felt independent and somewhat content. Most people can't wait to get away from the hospital, but to me it was almost like coming home. No one on the campus ever gave me strange looks, because they were accustomed to seeing people with burn injuries.

When I was subsequently offered a room at the Fisher House, a so-called comfort home on the grounds of BAMC, I jumped on it. Single troops normally weren't invited to stay there; it was geared toward families who needed to be close to their loved ones who were being treated. Fisher House 2, room 9, became my new home.

A couple of weeks later, I was sitting in my room when a box arrived for me. Inside were signed pairs of Nikes from Webber and Delk and a pair of Jordans from Bibby. Awesome.

I settled in for a long stay, because I was in line again for a major procedure. I'd talked with my plastic surgeon about addressing the cosmetics of my injury—I really wanted to have hair on my head. I didn't want to walk around for the rest of my life bald with my scalp grafts visible. I was so self-conscious about my head that I rarely left my room without wearing one of my many baseball caps, all in different colors representing different teams. I chose my hat each day to match my outfit.

The surgeon wanted to place an expander on my skull beneath the area where hair still grew. We could increase that section, he believed, to create more skin with hair follicles, which then could be used for the rest of my head. The expander would form a huge bubble and would stay implanted for about four months.

I'd seen pictures of other patients with head

expanders, and no way was I going out in public like that. I'd need to figure out how to cover it up. Also, the doctor was clear that, although the new skin could give me hair, it might not be the hair I once knew—it could be very thin and grow in different directions. I decided I didn't care. Hair is hair, and I had to have it (and I got it).

I also agreed to allow the surgeon to reimplant an expander in my chest, hoping for better results this time. The skin that grew from that site would be grafted onto the left side of my face, which was the most badly damaged area. Major surgery was required for both of these implants, so I asked my mother to come back to San Antonio for it.

Around summer 2004 a guy named Aaron was assigned to be my suitemate at Fisher House. Aaron, a twenty-four-year-old specialist from central California, had been a fuel truck driver in the Army. His accident occurred in Iraq about four months after mine. His vehicle, the second in a 173rd Airborne Brigade convoy on a supply run, was blasted by two rocket-propelled grenades. He suffered third-degree burns and a broken arm, among other injuries.

When I met Aaron, he was covered in skin grafts, several of his fingers had been amputated, and his hands curled into claws like mine. He was a smart guy, kind of quiet, and we spent a lot of time together hanging out—watching TV, usually. We amused ourselves with burn humor that we could never have expressed in front of other people, like how his truck had become a fireball after it was hit or how crazy my expanders made me look—comments that would only be funny to another burn survivor.

Many a night I'd use the bathroom we shared and accidentally leave the door on his side locked when I went to bed. In the middle of the night I'd hear Aaron banging on my door or ringing my phone to wake me up so he could use the toilet.

Although I liked having Aaron for company, sometimes his presence triggered my insecurities. When his girlfriend came from California to visit him, I knew enough to make myself scarce so they could have time to themselves. I'd sit in my easy chair, alone, and feel sorry for myself, grappling with surges of emotion brought on by a sad song or even a glimpse of myself in the mirror.

To ease those feelings, I'd jump in my car and drive aimlessly, the windows down and the music pumping to drown out my thoughts. Alternately, I'd take a quiet walk to the park.

I wouldn't call my mom for help. I knew I could, but I wouldn't. Little did I know, she was in a tough stage herself.

For some time, she'd been having a delayed reaction to my accident, and now she was in a downward spiral of depression and anxiety. This crisis had reminded her of so much she'd left behind years before.

My mom was born in 1956 in a rural village near Canton Carpintero in El Salvador, a tiny nation with the highest population density in Central America. People worked very hard, tending small plots for their rice, corn, and beans. They got their water for drinking and bathing not from faucets but from the river. They cooked by candlelight without the benefit of gas or electricity.

Staying healthy could be tricky and people were plagued by malnutrition and vitamin deficiencies and uncontrolled diseases such as malaria. With limited access to health care, Salvadorans frequently used house medicine to heal—a flower, a root, the bark from a tree. Sometimes these remedies worked; many times they didn't.

My mom was one of ten kids born to Paula Zavala, only six of whom lived past the age of four. My mom was "made in jail." Her father, Pio, had been behind bars for eighteen months for fighting and drunkenness; my grandmother visited him there and conceived my mother. My grandfather was still incarcerated when my mom was born, and he remained largely absent from her life thereafter.

My mother still remembers one night when she was a very little girl and a man burst through the front door of their home. She watched as the man, obnoxious and unsteady, lurched around the room. She was frightened of this loud, drunken stranger. The man lost his balance and went down at my mother's feet. She screamed as blood dripped from a cut on his chin.

"That's your daddy!" my grandmother hollered. "That's your daddy!"

Not long after this incident, my grandfather took up with another woman and moved with her to the neighboring nation of Honduras, leaving my grandmother with a houseful of kids. Overwhelmed and impoverished, my grandmother sent my mom to live with an adult niece named Angela and her man.

The couple was better off financially than my grandmother, but taking in the little girl wasn't an act of generosity. With no children of their own, they needed help with the chores. In exchange for room and board, the four-year-old was put to work minding the livestock. She milked the cows; fed the chickens and the pigs. For the next ten years her life was dominated by work and tears. There was no escape or distraction—no TV, no books save for the Bible, no toys. To this day, when anyone asks my mom what she'd like for Christmas, she requests dolls. She keeps them in a glass-front cabinet.

The community schoolteacher pressured Angela to register my mom for school. Reluctantly, the couple sent her off every morning, barefoot, minus the few centavos the students were prompted to bring for milk and crackers. My mom had to watch the other children eat their snack every day while she went without.

After finishing the third grade, my mom walked home clutching the certificate for entrance to the fourth grade. Someday, she thought, she might even go to college. But when the new school year began, Angela refused to buy my mom her uniforms or supplies. That was the end of my mom's formal instruction.

In a Catholic country where religion is paramount, Angela rarely took my mom to church and the little girl never received the first sacrament. She was left to learn about God by listening to other people discuss their faith. Craving the comfort of a spiritual life, she would gaze up at the clouds and pray, "Please, God, can you show me who you are?"

At fourteen, my mother was sent back to my grandmother's house, where the relentless chores continued. Her back ached from carrying buckets of water home from the river. She made soap for washing from the seed of the soap-nut tree and cooked on a wood fire against the wall of the house, preparing meals for the family and the field workers.

My grandmother never told her daughter she loved her, never offered a kiss or hug. She had a heavy hand and an even heavier tongue. Her nicknames for her oldest daughter weren't endearments such as "sweetie" or "honey," but bruising curses like "stupid" and "ugly." When my mom had a minute to herself, she'd sit beneath a tree and cry, asking God, "Why are you making me live here?" As her teenage years passed she listened for an answer, but none came.

Escape was all she could think about. When a young man from her village named Edelmiro showed interest, she thought he was her ticket out. She didn't particularly like him, but it didn't matter. The two of them ran far away to an orchard where Edelmiro could find work.

At twenty years old, my mom was finally out of the reach of her mother. She became pregnant, and by the time baby Maria Consuelo was just seventeen days old, it was clear that Edelmiro wasn't much of a provider or father. Defeated, my mom returned to my grandmother's house, stinging with the regret that her daughter would probably never know her father, just as my mom had never really known hers.

As though fate could sense her sadness, my mom got word that her father wanted to see her after all those years. Without a moment's hesitation, she bundled up infant Consuelo and hopped a bus for Honduras. My mom was elated to see her father and shocked to see how much she resembled him. *No wonder my mother is so mean to me,* she thought. *I remind her of this man she hates so much.*

The eight months my mother spent with her father and his partner, Lola, were some of the happiest days she'd ever known. As though making up for lost time, my grandfather lavished his daughter and her child with attention and affection. Maybe this could be her new life, my mom thought.

On New Year's Day 1978 my mother's Honduran respite came to a sudden end when her father was murdered by a drunken acquaintance who slashed him twenty-four times with a machete. Devastated and again without options, my mom returned to her mother's home in Carpintero, one-year-old Consuelo on her back. She found a job as a maid at a house in town, working for a teacher who paid my mom to cook and clean for the family of six. That job led to a better one, in San Salvador. She rode a dusty bus for five hours to the capital, leaving Consuelo with her grandmother.

Soon my mother allowed herself to be pulled off track by another man and became pregnant again. In this very Catholic part of the world, there was no birth control or sex education. If you were with a man, you were going to get pregnant. In September 1980 she gave birth to my second sister, Anabel.

The timing couldn't have been worse. A year earlier, a military junta had deposed President General Carlos Humberto Romero after years of human rights abuses by the government. Now the country was in the midst of a civil war that pitted the military-led government of El Salvador against the Farabundo Martí National Liberation Front (FMLN), a syndicate of left-wing guerrilla groups. In March, Archbishop Oscar Romero, a vocal opponent of the government's repression and use of violence against its citizens, had been assassinated while giving mass in a hospital; at his funeral, attended by more than a quarter of a million people, snipers had slaughtered dozens of mourners.

Two times my mother had found herself in the middle of a guerrilla shootout in San Salvador. Twice she'd had to drop to the floor, put her hands over her head, and pray for salvation.

With chaos all around and two little girls to raise, my mom managed to keep her heart full of hope. She decided she would go to America for a year to make enough money to open a business of her own later in El Salvador. Her mother agreed to look after my mom's girls while she was gone.

My mother found a coyote who was taking a group through Guatemala and Mexico to the United States for four hundred U.S. dollars, a steep sum for a woman who at best earned about one hundred dollars a month. But she managed to scrape it together from a relatively wealthy aunt, whom she would eventually repay, and a few neighbors, just in time for her departure on June 11, 1982.

At two o'clock that morning, she rose from her bed. She slid into one of the two dresses she owned, a blue one made of thin cotton, and folded a pair of jeans and a blouse into a shopping bag.

Two-year-old Anabel was sleeping, unaware that her own life was on the cusp of change. But Consuelo woke, sensing something was up.

"Mommy, where are you going?" she cried.

"I'm going to work, baby. Go back to sleep like a good girl and Mommy will bring you a pretty dress when I get back."

My mom tucked the little girl back into her bed and crept out. Her own mother didn't get up to say goodbye, instead calling, "God take care of you, wherever you are."

On June 30, having gone through pastures, deserts, and checkpoints; over hills and mountains; and across rivers that threatened to drown her, my mother, exhausted and frightened, arrived in Houston, Texas.

In September, she met Jose Martinez, and less than a year after that, I showed up.

Now, two decades and countless hardships later, my mom was finally buckling under the stress. Celestino seemed to be reaching his limit of concern for her. He told my mom that he didn't know what to do with her, which only made her push him away. After work one night she came home and fell asleep for a few hours.

She woke up and began a heart-to-heart with Celestino.

"I can't do this anymore," he told her. "Do you want me to bring you a priest or someone from our church?"

My mother told him she didn't want anybody to come. "I just want Jesus to come here and tell me why he's doing this to me."

Finally, Celestino said again, "I can't do this anymore." He'd already rented a new apartment.

Back at BAMC, my phone rang. It was my mom, and she sounded upset.

"What's wrong?" I asked her.

"I'll let Cele tell you," she said. I could hear her hand him the phone.

"It's too much," he said. "I try and try but I don't know what to do. I'm moving out."

I hadn't had any idea about the troubles at home. My mom hadn't let on.

"She needs you. You can't bail on her," I told Cele.

To my surprise, Celestino unpacked his suitcase and stayed. He continued to be the supportive partner she'd needed all along.

Maybe a year later I got quite a different phone call from my mom. She was giggling on the other end of the line. "Guess what we did!" she asked, like a kid calling to tell her dad that she'd gotten caught toilet-papering someone's house.

"What's up?"

"We got married at city hall!"

I was relieved and happy—they apparently were in a better place together. And now my mom would always have someone to lean on, I thought.

After the surgery to implant my expanders and after some time in the hospital post-op, I relaxed at the Fisher House with my mom, who had come back to BAMC to be with me for that operation. A few days later, public affairs invited me to attend an event in which a few troops from the hospital would be treated to lunch on the River Walk. A gentleman would be talking to the guys about an opportunity to start a nonprofit to help troops. A couple of our commanders asked me specifically to listen in to make sure none of our guys made any hasty decisions or commitments.

I stressed that I was recovering from surgery and didn't really feel up to it. They pressed, so I went.

We were all taken downtown in a van and dropped off at a hotel. I leaned up against a pillar in the lobby and listened as Doug Plank described his vision. With a partner, he wanted to start an organization that would assist service members. After he talked, we were directed to a boat for a lunch cruise.

My interest was piqued, and after the cruise ended, I stayed behind to speak with Doug. I wanted to share my insights and see whether they meshed with his ideas. I told him about my mother; I wanted to close the financial gap for families who were summoned to the hospital to be with their loved ones and the economic blow they took doing so. My mom obviously couldn't work—and therefore didn't earn any money—when she was by my side in San Antonio. She had struggled to pay her rent, utilities, and other bills. She'd had to rely on my income from the Army and help from Celestino to subsidize her time by my side.

Our family's tight situation hadn't gone unnoticed by the community of Dalton. A woman named Mary Rose Threet, whose son Jeffeory had been the kicker on my football team, instituted a support fund at a local bank, inviting any and all donations. They poured in. It was overwhelming for both of us to witness the generosity of our neighbors, especially when I'd lived there for only one year before I enlisted.

But what about families whose communities didn't or couldn't step up like this? Every family was saddled with the extra worry of financial pressures brought on by their absence from work and home.

I told Doug I wanted to help raise money to assist these families. I also mentioned that the Department of Defense sometimes covered only the first flight to the hospital and back. If the family member went home and then wanted to return to the hospital, the airfare often came out of their own pocket. (To be fair and accurate: Remember, I was injured at the beginning of the war, and the DoD was working to resolve many of these issues.)

Doug agreed with all my concerns. I emphasized that I would do whatever I could, in any way, to help.

"You're really good at communicating," he said. "You could be a spokesman."

Spokesman. I liked the way that sounded, although I didn't really know what it meant.

Doug tried to explain. "You'll go out and talk to people about the organization, meet with potential donors."

Great idea, I thought. *I can do this!*

I spoke with Doug nearly every other day for months, staying up-to-date on the proposed direction of the nonprofit, which was tentatively called the Coalition to Salute America's Heroes. I continued to do interviews every time public affairs asked, so I felt that I was making strides with this media stuff.

That was on the outside. On the inside, I was still the same lonely guy.

I felt embarrassed to be seen in public with my expanders, so I tried to hide in my room when I could. Norma Guerra, the public affairs chief, noticed. It was her responsibility to keep her eye on the troops, like me, who sometimes did press for the facility. Passing me in the hallway one day, she asked, "Why are you in your room all the time?" I didn't have an answer for her. She approached my commander. "I have a job for Martinez," she told him. "He needs to report to my office."

So I did, every morning, five days a week. I'd get there at around nine and eat my breakfast at the receptionist's desk, my new post. The phones were always ringing off the hook.

"BAMC public affairs, Specialist Martinez," I'd say.

Sometimes it was a small-town newspaper reporter at the other end, requesting an interview with one of their own. Or it might be a Girl Scout troop leader in Cincinnati, asking where to send the get-well cards her girls had made. Sometimes calls came from the offices of dignitaries and high-ranking officers; sometimes it was a major media outlet.

I helped set up tours, escorted media around BAMC, organized and distributed donations, and advised other soldiers before their press appearances. I even was issued a BAMC Public Affairs Office badge. I still spent time with patients, usually in the afternoon, in between my PAO obligations.

Inadvertently, Norma was paving the way for my future. When reporters called our office requesting an interview with a wounded soldier, she usually recommended me for the job. The staff taught me the ropes both in front of and behind the camera. I began to feel more and more comfortable in interview situations. I learned to choose my words carefully when answering a reporter's questions. I had a sense that people respected me for doing these interviews. Honestly, I felt like the shit. I was the dude dealing with high officials and important press. Some of the other patients started calling me "Hollywood." (I didn't like that then and I don't like it now.)

People began to call Norma my "Texas mom." Although we differed on one crucial element— she was a San Antonio Spurs fan and I was not —she and I became very close.

Sometimes her son, Brian, who's my age, came over to BAMC. We liked to hang out together and later became good friends. When my mom and I attended the Daytime Emmy Awards in 2009 (I was a cast member of *All My Children* by then), Norma designed and sewed the dress my mom wore.

My mom couldn't always make it back out to San Antonio for some of my smaller surgeries, so she'd ask Norma to look in on me to make sure everything went okay. Norma would show up early in the morning before I was taken into the OR. Afterward, she would visit me in the recovery room with a peanut butter and banana sandwich and an orange Gatorade, which would ease my post-surgery nausea.

The thing about Norma that I appreciated most was that she knew how to get me good. After one surgery, she pleaded with the doctor ahead of time to tell her which recovery room I'd be sent to. When I opened my eyes, fresh out of anesthesia, I was shocked by the sight of San Antonio Spurs insignia plastered all over the walls. The staff cracked up when the first words I uttered were, "I've died and gone to hell."

On another occasion, there was a senator scheduled to come visit BAMC. The general wanted some of us troops to meet her and show her around. Norma told each of us that the senator was a huge Spurs fan so, on the general's orders, Norma would be supplying us all with Spurs T-shirts and hats that we were required to wear. I didn't take kindly to this directive, but once I understood that the other guys had agreed to wear the gear, I reluctantly got on board.

On the appointed day at the appointed time, I walked into the conference room, wearing my Spurs fan memorabilia. I was the only one. The other troops were in uniform. I looked over at Norma. She just grinned. She'd gotten me again.

Practical jokes aside, Norma really looked out for me. In the public affairs office there was a large wall-mounted whiteboard behind my desk on which the staff would write reminders and scheduling notes. One morning during a lull, Norma sat down in a chair in front of me.

I had decided to figure out a new way to sign my name. Someday I might be signing important papers, and I wanted to do so in style. I spent half a day signing and signing on that whiteboard, practicing my *J*, trying to come up with the perfect signature. Norma critiqued each idea.

The coalition finally got off the ground and began to pursue its mission of helping troops. I was suddenly surrounded by well-spoken, educated people. I became interested in learning to communicate better, to use words that would really captivate others. I began to pay attention to the way I talked, to my grammar, to my accent.

Doug made good on his suggestion that I serve as one of the spokesmen, and although my participation wasn't sanctioned by BAMC, they were aware that I volunteered with the coalition.

Doug sent me and the other volunteers to media training in the coalition's PR offices outside Washington, D.C. They put us in a room and fired questions at us. I practiced my answers, trying to figure out how to condense my words to get out more of our message.

My expanders were removed and another round of grafting surgery was completed in July 2004. I got lots of on-the-job training doing interviews for BAMC, and the coalition began to send me to speak for them around the country. I felt that I had a natural affinity for what I was doing, and others apparently thought so as well, as I soon was the go-to guy for interviews for the coalition. I was able to communicate the goals of the organization well, and my scars added credence to my message. I started receiving specific invitations from news personalities, such as Fox's Neil Cavuto; I became a regular contributor on his show, *Your World with Neil Cavuto*.

In late summer the coalition execs began to plan their first annual retreat in Florida for wounded troops and their families and were casting about for the event's entertainment. They had some names but no real leads. When someone donated some tickets to a few BAMC troops for the Toby Keith concert in August in San Antonio, and I was lucky enough to get one, it occurred to me that the singer would be the perfect person to perform at our event.

Doug said, "Do your best."

A guy named Dan Vargas, an airman from Randolph Air Force Base, frequently volunteered to accompany wounded troops to events in town, and he escorted our group to the venue. Dan is a big teddy bear of a guy, about twenty years older than me.

On the drive over to the event, I told Dan about my Toby Keith idea.

"Go for it," he said.

At the concert, the other wounded troops and I had a little meet-and-greet with Toby and his band. I gave my elevator pitch about the coalition to Toby and then spoke to one of his handlers.

A week or two later, the band's management was in negotiations with the coalition. In December, Toby Keith performed at our event in Florida.

Deborah Norville, the broadcaster from my hometown, had heard my story in September and invited me to appear on her show. A limo picked me up at LaGuardia Airport in New York and took me to my room at the Hilton on Sixth Avenue. I'd never been in such a beautiful hotel. My room was on a high floor with windows overlooking midtown Manhattan. I immediately ducked out to explore the city. That evening a stretch limo picked me up and transported me to the studios on West Fifty-Seventh Street for my interview.

I loved New York—the energy, the important events going on in that city, the powerful people. I wondered how it felt to live there. I could barely contain myself.

I called Norma back in San Antonio to brag. "Guess where I am? New York City!"

"What?" she yelled. "You're not supposed to be that far away from this hospital!"

I was active duty, and soldiers need permission

from their command to travel beyond a fifty-mile radius of their duty station. I was about seven hundred miles over that limit.

"You'd better get back here fast," she warned me, "before people start looking for you."

When I returned, someone indeed had been looking for me—the hospital's commanding general. I was summoned to his office, escorted over from Fisher House by my captain on one side of me, a sergeant major on the other, and a sergeant behind me. I looked like a prisoner being walked to the electric chair, although I wasn't really worried.

"I flip on the TV and I see you talking about the coalition," the general said, as I stood at attention in front of his desk. "I thought we had all discussed this."

I was a specialist and he was a general, but I knew he liked me, and in my mind, we were buds. I was absurdly cocky.

"Yes, sir," I returned. "But I'm not asking people for money. I'm just talking about the organization. People can make up their own minds. We're living this—at my home there's bills and my mom has bad credit now."

He told me that he understood what I was trying to do but that I was walking a very fine line—that I needed to be careful and speak to the public affairs office any time I had an opportunity to represent the coalition. I didn't listen. I believed in what I was doing and why I was doing it, and I vowed to do anything the coalition asked.

And they asked a lot. Several times a month beginning in the fall of 2004, a black town car would pull up curbside to the hospital. I'd emerge from my room, trailing a small suitcase containing my suit.

"Mr. Martinez?" the driver would ask.

"That's me," I'd say, hopping into the back, aware of the eyes on me.

The car would speed down I-35, depositing me at the San Antonio airport, where I'd take a flight to New York for some sort of press event or to D.C. to meet with the coalition's media team or executives. And to think I'd never even owned a suit before.

Back in high school, the football team wore slacks, a tie, and a sport coat on game days. When I enlisted, my dress uniform became my suit. But I needed to look sharp to represent the coalition, and the administrators told me to purchase some clothes on their dime, so my mom and I went to a Men's Wearhouse in Chattanooga and I chose a few suits.

I felt good when I put them on. I almost felt like I didn't have any scars. Sometimes I even forgot I had them. I'd think about the suit and the reason I was wearing it. It made me feel powerful. Maybe I wasn't 100 percent confident about my face and body, but I was doing so well in other ways that it offset the looks. It was cool to be going to a lunch meeting with grown-ass men who had been doing this stuff for a lot longer than me.

People told me I should run for office. Yup, they really did. I was a twenty-one-year-old kid.

And I was the big man on campus again.

CHAPTER TWELVE

Getting Back on the Bike

In the spring of 2005 I got word that I was going to be moved from the Fisher House to the barracks next to the hospital. I was relieved to learn I'd have a single room. I wasn't yet comfortable living with people with other types of injuries and baring my scars for all eyes to see.

In the meantime, I continued to hone my speaking skills. In addition to volunteering with the coalition, I sometimes answered requests to tell my story before church groups or other audiences.

And then it was time for me to begin the Army Medical Evaluation Board process. When a disabled soldier goes before the board, his or her medical evidence is researched so that a disability rating can be assigned. The evaluation usually takes about nine months to complete. The Army had started asking me to begin the process about seven months after my injury occurred.

No, I kept telling them. There was no way I was getting out of the Army and potentially sacrificing the care I needed.

But now I felt ready. The board took photos of all my injuries and scars and questioned me about my current abilities. I was concerned that I'd be assigned a low rating, which I'd have to appeal. I needn't have worried: I was satisfied with the board's decision.

While I was waiting for my percentage to be calculated, I needed something to fill my time. I'd made friends with a couple of other burn-unit patients, so now I had people my own age to hang out with. One day I was driving around town with my friend R.C., who had been burned in Iraq and had lost an eye and some fingers. I saw a store on the side of the road that advertised quads and minibikes.

"R.C., pull over!"

We went inside the store, spoke to the salesman for a while and, before you know it, we had each plunked down $600 for our own minibikes. Never mind that a special permit was required to drive them.

We brought those minibikes back to Fort Sam Houston and laughed ourselves silly driving them at top speeds around the base. We'd fly around the corner by the medical center, competing to see which of us could get to the highest speeds. More than once, the military police came after us, but we usually managed to evade them by hiding behind Dumpsters or parked cars.

R.C. and I, along with a kid named Archie and a

nineteen-year-old from El Paso named Sam, were together a lot, both on base and off. We shared an interest in customized cars. I still had my gold Maxima, R.C. got a black Ford Ranger, Archie had a black Nissan Xterra, and once Sam had saved up his money, he bought a Toyota Celica.

The four of us went to car shows together. Sometimes we'd drive all the way to Dallas, nearly three hundred miles away, for one. We poked around auto supply stores looking for speakers and other cool gear for the cars. We shopped online together, too. We surrounded ourselves with the world of custom cars.

One day I was driving around and pulled into a car shop advertising: "Our specialty is air suspension." I thought that sounded cool, and it was. Even better: The shop hosted a car club for guys like us.

I started hanging out at that shop nearly every day. Before too long, I'd painted and gutted my Nissan and installed two televisions in it.

I became tight with a guy named Jason, a civilian who hung out at the shop. I was pleased to have a friend outside of the military. On weekends, we'd go cruising downtown. We'd drive down Commerce Street, past the bars and restaurants and over to a section called Market Square, and then back up a street called Market. For hours and hours. We'd be at a traffic light and hear a dude pull up next to us, our car vibrating from the thump of his speakers. It was like Battle of the Bands.

After we got tired of that, we'd get something to eat and go home—back to BAMC—to our beds. Sometimes we'd go to Hooters, but that was about as racy as it got. None of these guys did drugs or drank a whole lot. It was good, clean fun.

You'd think my body had been through enough, but in 2005 I decided to get the first of two tattoos. I was hanging out with R.C., bored, when he decided he'd get a tattoo to honor some of the guys he'd served with who'd lost their lives. The two of us went to a tattoo place, and while we were there, I decided to get one, too. In truth, I'd always wanted one that acknowledges the love between me, my mother, and my two sisters. The artist drew up a design and inked it onto my right calf. It's a flower, a cross, and a heart intertwined, with all of our names: Maria, Consuelo, Anabel, and J.R.

The tattoo you've more likely seen on me is the watch on my left wrist. I got it in 2008, when I'd just turned twenty-five. I'd gone skydiving for my birthday, but I wanted to mark my quarter century in a more permanent way.

During my first days at Fort Campbell, one of my sergeants would ask me for the time. I could never remember military time, which operates off a twenty-four-hour clock. So I'd answer "two o'clock" instead of "fourteen hundred," or whatever, and I'd get smoked for it. As soon as I could afford it I bought an inexpensive Army watch so I wouldn't get stuck anymore.

The day I was hurt, I was wearing that watch. My entire hand and arm was burned except for the wrist beneath the watch.

My tattoo's watch face is zigzagged, signifying that it is broken. The hands read two thirty, which is the time I was injured. And the date of the explosion is written in roman numerals on the band.

On my way to the tattoo parlor I called my mom. "Hey, I'm getting another tattoo," I told her. "And by the way, out of curiosity, what time of day was I born?"

"It was two thirty in the afternoon," she told me.

I was born and reborn at the same time.

As optimistic as I felt most days, and as much as I tried to lead a "normal" life, the concern about whether I'd ever find a mate who would love me the way I was now was never far from my mind. Sometimes the boys and I went out to clubs to go dancing. Girls would talk to me, be sociable, but their friendliness never extended to personal interest. It was pretty painful.

There was this one waitress at our hangout bar—her name was Amanda. She was light-skinned with dark hair, a really beautiful girl. I wanted to talk to her so bad, but I couldn't bring myself to do it. My friends dared me, night after night, until I finally did. She was friendly, but I knew there wasn't anything there. When I worked up the nerve to ask her for her number, she put me off. The handful of girls who did show interest in me weren't people I was attracted to.

I was monumentally afraid of rejection, so I'd go out on the dance floor and dance by myself. I'd put myself in the middle of a big circle and do the robot and other stupid moves. At closing time, I'd always head back to the barracks alone. Sometimes I'd be upset.

And then things changed.

I was in a club downtown with my friends. The crowd in the bar was a bit older. Like always, I started dancing by myself. I spotted a cute girl across the dance floor. She was watching me, so I smiled at her to gauge her interest. She smiled back. Before you know it, she was dancing with me, and by the end of the night, we were making out in the bar. I was thrilled—here I was with this beauty, someone whom any of my friends would want to be with. We exchanged numbers and I left feeling like the shit.

She texted me from the car: "You're a great dancer. Can't wait to hang out again!"

Jennifer was twenty-six. She lived with her parents about forty-five minutes away from town. Allegedly. She was divorced, didn't have any kids, and had a regular nine-to-five job. Allegedly. We talked on the phone every other night, and it felt good.

I told my friends at the car shop all about her, but they didn't believe me. "Yeah, right," they said, because they'd never seen her. A few times she told me she was going to come over to the barracks and hang out with me. I'd get all excited—I wanted to show her off to my friends —but she never came.

Still, we did manage to get together for a few dates. One of those nights was epic for me, because it was the first time I bared all my scars to a grown woman—not a girl—and an experienced one at that.

At the same time, it tore me down, because she really didn't seem to care about me. I finally realized that she was playing with me. There was something slippery about her, and I didn't want to be part of it. I ended it, and I found myself feeling bitter about girls. I knew I had something to offer, but the only attributes that truly interested women, I felt, were looks or money.

I told my mom about my newfound convictions.

"You have to stop pushing girls away," she said. "You might be pushing the right one away. If you don't open yourself up, you're going to be lonely. You don't give people a chance."

I did give people a chance, but it irritated me

when girls looked right past me or, alternately, sidled up to me and told me they'd seen me on TV doing my BAMC or coalition work, as if I could do something for them. It put a sour taste in my mouth.

"Mama didn't raise no fool," my mother said. "But you need to open your heart, and also open your ears and eyes. Ears, so you can hear when people tell you to be careful of a certain girl, and eyes to see for yourself."

I reminded her that I only had one ear. She laughed.

"Okay," I said. "Maybe you're right." I vowed to change my attitude.

I was still hanging around with Jason and the other car-loving guys. Jason knew a few girls who lived in Dallas, so a couple of us hopped in our cars and cruised up there one weekend to see them. It was there that I met Renee. She was African-American, a good dancer, and a whole lot of fun. We hung out that weekend and stayed in touch when I went back to BAMC.

In December 2005 my service member's traumatic injury insurance policy finally paid out, and I suddenly had more cash than I'd ever seen. Now I didn't just feel like *the* shit, I felt like King Shit. R.C. had gotten his payout, too, and we started going to Dallas a lot. I wanted to be the big man, so when we went to a bar, I'd pay for everyone's drinks. We'd go to a restaurant, and I'd pick up the tab. I'd never had the resources to do that before, and it felt great.

That payout also gave me the opportunity to do something I'd always dreamed about. I knew my mom continued to struggle, and God knows I understood the sacrifices she'd made for me my whole life. I wanted to take care of her. To me, the best way to do that was to help her buy a home.

"Start looking," I told her.

She couldn't believe it. She and Cele went house hunting just like regular Americans everywhere, and she ended up finding one she fell in love with on a pretty grass-lined road within the Dalton city limits. It was a brand-new two-story brick colonial with a small garden in the back. I put up the down payment, we bought some furniture, and my mom moved in with Celestino. I claimed one of the bedrooms as my own, and after a while I asked my uncle to move in. I guess I just wanted us all to be a family.

On March 16, 2006, I was medically retired from the Army. I still wanted to serve, but I wanted it to be on my own terms. After my release, I went home for a couple of weeks. For the past four years my mom had been asking me when we were going to spend some time together. I frequently used my convalescent leave to travel for the coalition, and she was feeling neglected. And I wanted to be there for her.

That month I went to Cancun with R.C. and Jason to celebrate retirement. We had a blast doing what everyone does on spring break. The surf! The girls! The parties! The only downer for me was that I was too embarrassed to take off my shirt on the beach. Now it wasn't only the scars but the spare tire I lugged around, too. After I saw the photos from the trip, I said, "Oh my God, I'm big!" I'd ballooned to 240 pounds. That wasn't going to work anymore.

When I got back to Dalton, I told my mom that things needed to change. "Don't make me lasagna or any of that stuff," I said. "I'm eating healthy."

I researched how to lose weight and what foods to avoid. I went at it like a full-time job. I wouldn't eat anything after six thirty in the evening. I drank a boatload of water. I went to the gym first thing in the morning and did the elliptical like a madman. Later in the afternoon I'd grab a couple of my mom's dogs—she has six little dachshund mixes!—and go for a run. And it worked.

But I really felt the deficit of opportunity acutely. Some of my friends in Dalton weren't doing a whole lot of anything. I had my friends in Texas now, and the coalition was based on the East Coast. R.C.—who'd recently retired from the Army as well—and I had been talking about moving to Dallas, and now we cemented those plans.

In July, we rented an apartment together in Big D. It was the first time I'd been on my own, really on my own, without the supervision of the Army. Once I no longer was active duty, I could work full-time for the coalition. My job didn't really change, but the fact that I was now able to accept compensation and support myself made a big difference in my psyche.

In the meantime, I continued to make a name for myself as a speaker. People reacted positively to me, which boosted my confidence. In 2006 I met a gentleman named Dave Roever, who had been burned beyond belief in the Vietnam War. Dave had since created a faith-based foundation and had turned his experiences into inspiration. He invited me to travel with him on his private jet, and we went to churches and military bases in Florida, Kentucky, Colorado, Texas—wherever Dave was requested. He'd introduce me—"I'd like to bring out a friend of mine"—and I'd speak for ten or fifteen minutes.

Working with Dave offered me the invaluable experience of learning how to fine-tune my message to fit a narrow time frame. I figured out how to get an audience excited. I wasn't proclaiming to be a self-help guru, but my message was that we're all fighters and we're all courageous and we can all make it through hardship.

As great as it was to work with Dave, I began to want to be the headliner instead of the opening act. I realized that I needed an agent or a representative, someone to help me with my developing career. But everyone I found wanted to see a demo reel or a packet, which would include a cover letter outlining my experience, a head shot, and a résumé. I didn't have any of those. So I continued to rely on word of mouth for speaking gigs.

Now that I was in her city, Renee and I started to hang out a lot, too. She had a boyfriend, so technically the two of us were just friends, but we kept getting closer. I liked being around her because she was open to doing lots of things, and I have that kind of personality, too. We loved to go to a sports bar and arcade in town. We'd play laser tag and pool, have drinks and dance. On her twenty-second birthday—after she had become single again—I delivered twenty-two doughnuts to her apartment.

It was a good relationship, but I was still defensive. When I caught her in a little lie, my emotional fences began to rise. Trust is such a big thing with me, and I didn't want anyone else playing games with me.

"If you tell me a lie about something small," I told her, "you'll definitely lie about something big."

In December 2006 the Coalition to Salute America's Heroes put on its annual conference in Orlando, which I attended. I hooked up with a girl working for one of the vendors. Her name was Sarah. She was a cute girl, Caucasian, with dark hair and pretty eyes. We ended up hanging out for the entire conference, keeping it on the down-low so that no eyebrows were raised. I was mad at Renee for lying and was pretty much over her, so I didn't feel guilty. Sarah and I already were crazy about each other by the time the conference ended.

Sarah was the first girl I really loved. She wasn't in a relationship, so she was free to love me back. She was smart and had a great job. She had an air of mystery about her that always made me want to know more.

But she lived in the Southeast and I lived in Dallas. I wanted to be around her all the time and it sucked that we lived so far apart. The good news, though, was that via my continuous travel for the coalition I was able to swing it so Sarah and I could see each other about twice a month. When we were together, it felt so good. I was in heaven.

But sometimes I felt like I wasn't getting the whole story from her, like she was keeping some kind of secret from me. I wondered why she still shared a car insurance policy with her former boyfriend. In fact, I wondered why she was still in touch with him at all. With my trust issues, those questions bothered me, but I couldn't get answers from her. It got to the point where we were fighting all the time. After about fifteen months,

I decided I couldn't take it anymore. "I'm stepping away so you can figure it out," I told her. "Let me know when you want to be honest." I loved her and believed she loved me, too, but I needed to feel confident about our relationship.

In the spring of 2007 Cele lost his job and my mom and my uncle were having trouble meeting the mortgage without Cele's income. I couldn't afford to pay for my apartment in Dallas and cover the Dalton mortgage, too, so I decided to move back to Georgia. I didn't want to, but I didn't really think I had a choice.

So by the end of the summer in 2007, there I was. I felt defeated. Not only was I back home under my mom's wing, but I had struck out in the love department again.

One day my mom asked me, "How's Sarah?"

I sat next to her on the couch and began to cry big racking sobs. "Sarah and I broke up," I told her. I felt like I couldn't breathe, it hurt so bad.

My mom hugged me, told me how sorry she was. It was one of the few times when there wasn't anything she could do to help me.

Then in early 2008 I received a much-needed morale boost. I'd recently met a *People* correspondent who had been searching for candidates for a story that would commemorate the fifth anniversary of the Iraq War. She pitched me to her editors, and I was one of the subjects chosen for the piece. I got a nice write-up accompanied by a full-page color portrait. This break gave me back some of the hope I'd lost. I knew the exposure could bring me more speaking opportunities— or an agent might even come calling.

And months later, Sarah finally gave me the answers to my questions. She told me her secret: She was addicted to pain medication and her ex-boyfriend was her supplier. She said she was going to get help, and she did. After a few months, I felt secure enough to try again with her. We began to talk about moving in together. I felt that it was important for her to leave her hometown so we could start fresh, and she agreed. We talked about Charleston, Atlanta. I thought Los Angeles or New York. We searched the Internet for apart-ments.

Then we started arguing again. I didn't feel like I had her whole heart. In September 2008 I traveled to her city for a coalition event. I hadn't told her I was coming, but when I arrived I really wanted to see her. So I called her. She didn't answer. I called and called, leaving message after message. She never answered, never phoned back.

I finally had to accept that the relationship wasn't going to work. I was heartbroken, and I needed something to bring me up, bring me out.

And then, the world of make-believe came calling.

CHAPTER THIRTEEN

Welcome to Hollywood

"You know, one day I'm going to be on one of these shows," I told my mom. We were spending our day in the usual way: me in my ICU bed, she in a chair next to me, watching Spanish telenovelas. They bored me. The acting seemed so over the top, and I couldn't understand why they dragged out each story line when the answers to their problems seemed so clear.

My mom tore her gaze away from the TV. "Oh, really?"

Actually, it was more of a statement than a question. "Yup, I have the story line planned out in my head," I said.

She turned her body toward me. I had her attention.

"There's going to be a guy who's with this beautiful girl," I started. "One day he gets burned in a car accident, and when the girlfriend shows up at the hospital to see him, it's going to be me. She helps me to get better, and then we happily run off into the sunset together."

She yawned and blinked.

I continued. "I would be perfect for the role because I won't require any makeup to make it believable. I can show up and go straight to work."

She giggled appreciatively and turned back to the novela.

It's true, I really did think about this. I started to imagine it. I was going to single-handedly smash the stereotype of Hollywood as the world of perfect people.

One Friday morning five years later I was sound asleep in a hotel room in Los Angeles after visiting a friend. My BlackBerry buzzed on the bedside table. *Who the hell could be calling me at this time of the morning?* I thought irritably. It buzzed and dinged and vibrated until finally I gave in and picked up the offending little device.

I opened my email and saw a bunch of forwarded mails from my friend Dan Vargas. I wondered why he was forwarding me a damn email chain. I hate them. They usually end with an admonition to forward to ten of your friends to avoid a string of bad luck. I usually just delete them without reading them so I don't invite that penalty.

Dan was the guy who had escorted the veterans to that Toby Keith concert a few years back. Since that time, he'd become executive director for Operation Finally Home, a nonprofit that provides mortgage-free houses for the severely wounded returning from Afghanistan and Iraq. Back in 2007, Dan had called me out on my residual anger and fear and how those emotions were eating me up. He told me straight-out, "The only one who's going to help J.R. is J.R."

In the intervening years, he'd become my best friend. Which meant he should have known not to call me so early.

My phone rang again. "It's seven a.m., man. What's up?"

He asked me if I'd read any of the emails he'd sent me.

I told him I hadn't.

"You have to look at them now," he said. "Call me back."

The emails were a casting call for a daytime drama. Producers were interested in adding an injured veteran from Afghanistan or Iraq to the story line. I read this and jerked up from the pillow.

I was perfect for this job. I marveled about the whole notion. Who would've thought this up? How would it happen?

When a new character is introduced into the story line of a show, the writers come up with a scenario and character descriptions. The casting director sends out the word to agents who might have clients who fit the bill. Once résumés begin to arrive, the casting director sifts through them and brings in matches. A series of auditions narrows the pool until it's down to about twenty hopefuls.

At that point the executive producer is called in to review the candidates, and he or she usually will choose about four or five finalists. They are invited to come to the studio to test against the actors they'll be playing opposite. The executives are looking for someone who has that special sparkle on camera. Then the network weighs in and the person is chosen.

All My Children was the show that was casting. This fan favorite—about the residents of a make-believe East Coast suburb called Pine Valley—had been running for more than forty years. I knew all about it; my mom was a fan and I'd grown up with that show on our television.

All My Children's head writer had hit on an idea to introduce a story about an Iraq veteran. The executive producer, Julie Carruthers, quickly agreed, and they decided to go with a real veteran—someone who probably hadn't acted previously—rather than try to fake an injury. Let's put out a call, she told Judy, the casting director, and see what kind of response we get. Within weeks the casting office had received more than six hundred submissions. Just about every after-noon, Judy headed over to Julie's office, where she'd sink down on the couch and vent about all the sad stories she was reading. Nearly all the veterans who applied were amputees. The producers hadn't even considered showcasing a burned veteran.

Judy weeded the stack down to about twenty-five veterans. In the meantime, I'd received the email from Dan, so I called the casting offices in New York. Impossibly, I got the casting director on the phone on the first try.

"The character is a guy called Brot Monroe," she said.

The more I talked, the more Judy listened, and finally she invited me to meet her.

"For me to even consider you," she said, "you need to come to New York."

No problem. "I'll be in New York next week." I actually would be; I was attending a speakers' conference to learn how to amplify my speaking career.

"Can you stop in?" she asked.

The morning of our meeting I dressed carefully: a pair of gray slacks and a light pink long-sleeved shirt.

Judy met me in the lobby and we went into her office. I told her more details about my injury. I'd gotten pretty good at telling my story. She seemed interested. I got the vibe that she liked me.

"Hold on," she said. "I'm going to see if the executive producer can come down here to meet you." She got on the phone and dialed the number to Julie's office. "Ask Julie if she can come down here to meet one of the candidates for the Brot role," she told the assistant, Diana Gonzalez-Jones. She turned back to me. "She only has a second, but she's going to shoot down here."

Julie walked into the office and, as she told me at the end of that brief meeting, "Within less than sixty seconds, I was in love. But still," she said, "at the end of the day we're going to have to put you on camera and see what you look like."

"That's great," I told her. "Even if I'm not the right person for you, I would love to help tell the story." As I said that, I was confident I'd do well.

After the meeting I walked over to Lincoln Center and called my mom. She was so excited for me. I had a really good feeling in my heart that I had a shot at it.

Back home in Dalton, I continued to work out and eat healthily. I watched *All My Children* every day.

"Mom, I'm going to watch my stories," I'd say. If I did get this part, I needed to know what was going on in Pine Valley.

In mid-September I returned to New York for my screen test. I was nervous, but I willed myself to project the self-assurance I knew the producers wanted to see in a potential actor.

After they'd pretty much decided on me, the producers, writers, and execs from the network discussed whether I'd be okay on camera, whether the audience would be able to accept my burn scars.

A week or so later, on a Friday, I got a call from Julie telling me I had the part. My guardian angel had come through once again: It happened to be Anabel's birthday.

"Thank you so much!" I shouted into the phone. "Thank you, thank you, thank you!" And I said a silent thanks to Anabel.

"Look, here's the thing," Julie told me. "You have that special something that's going to be successful with an audience, but you're not an actor. You're going to tell the story for the people serving our country. That's going to have a huge impact."

I'll work my ass off, I told her. "I want you to be hard on me. Tell me if I suck. But I'm going to make this the best thing you ever had on this show."

After we hung up, I called my mom. I wanted to mess with her. "Mom, *All My Children* just called," I said with a sad voice.

"Oh, niño, I'm sorry. It's okay," she said.

I paused for a minute, and then hollered, "I got the job!"

She screamed her high-pitched scream. "For real?"

"Yes, Mom!"

It would be a three-month gig. We decided on a start date a couple of weeks away, in October 2008. The show would put me up in a hotel until I could find an apartment. The hotel was ten blocks away from the studio, which was on Sixty-Sixth Street and West End Avenue on the Upper West Side.

Julie asked me to get on the phone with the writer to tell him my story. So I spent a lot of time with him, telling him all about what happened, the showers and scrubbing, the depression and pain, and all about my mother. The writer brought many of those memories to life. The larger challenge for me as an actor would be to make the connection to events that were fictional.

In addition to the intangibles, I also had to quickly learn about the other elements that go into a performance, from wardrobe fittings to camera blocking. The one thing I didn't have to endure was hair and makeup, as I only required a little bit of anti-shine and powder. And that wasn't even all the time. I considered myself lucky. I'd always thought that only rock 'n' roll superstars wore eyeliner but no, here at *All My Children* I found that some of the guys wore it. Some even had abs sprayed on them for their love scenes.

It was a whole new world. It wasn't the way I thought it would be. And oddly enough, it was exactly what I thought it would be.

On my first day on the set, *Good Morning America* was scheduled to come in and follow me around, documenting my virgin voyage. When the *All My Children* producers had warned this would happen, what could I say, except, "Okay, cool!" As if I didn't already have enough pressure in one day.

An assistant showed me to my dressing room—nope, my name wasn't on it. On the way, I passed Susan Lucci, daytime's reigning goddess, as she headed to hair and makeup. I went crazy in my mind but I managed to play it cool. She smiled at me and I smiled back. I didn't say anything.

I stayed in my dressing room reading my lines until I was mustered to sit down for an interview with *GMA*. The character of Brot was an Iraq War vet who pretended to have died in action rather than let the woman he loved, a fellow soldier, see him covered with scars.

Shortly before I was due for my first scene, I was approached by one of the show's seasoned actors with whom I'd be sharing my acting debut.

"Hey, babe," he said. That's what he called everyone. "Do you want to run lines by the window?"

We had about twenty minutes to go before I was due on set. "Sure," I said. "But what does that mean?"

"It means do you want to practice our lines?" he said.

I did. But instead of looking at the script, this actor started telling me his life story. Before I knew it, our twenty minutes were up. Somehow, I managed to get through my first scenes okay anyway. I could do it—I'd done it. I hadn't messed anything up.

As if to underscore that certainty, a bunch of new scripts had been stacked in the mailbox mounted on the door of my dressing room. Apparently the writers were excited about the new character of Brot, so they wrote a lot of dialogue for him. I spent every waking moment going over my lines. Luckily I have a good memory; otherwise, I don't know how people do it.

I probably did ten to fifteen shows in the first two weeks. It was a huge amount of work, but I was exhilarated. I wanted to know everything that was going on on the set, and I was determined to learn everyone else's lines. That way if something was changed in the script, I'd know what was happening in the action.

Every night I'd buy myself a foot-long Subway sandwich, go back to my hotel room, and read my lines over and over. I'd eat half the sandwich and keep the other half to take to work the next day. I needed to save my money to pay for the apartment I hoped to get soon. And within a few weeks, I'd signed a year lease. I was that sure of myself. I bought a couch, a bed, a TV, and a table and chairs from IKEA.

I spent a lot of time going back and forth between the studios and the show's administrative offices to speak to the producers. Julie's assistant was half African-American and half Puerto Rican, a former honors student from Queens, and the daughter of a police officer. She'd graduated from St. John's University and gone straight to work in this industry. I had to go through Diana any time I wanted to speak to Julie. I didn't mind—Diana was friendly and easy on the eyes. She was slim with big curly hair and dark almond eyes. She was independent and strong and I could usually crack her up.

I found myself hanging around up there even when I didn't have a real reason. Diana and I would chat about random stuff: my scene that day, what she was doing over the weekend, my mom, her sisters.

"We gotta hang out," she said.

I told one of my friends, "I'd marry that girl in a heartbeat, but she's not interested in me that way."

My life still was pretty one-dimensional, consisting of work and home. Occasionally I'd go out at night and duck into a bar for a drink, but I never met anyone, didn't really talk to anybody. I could walk around the city anonymously because my story line hadn't begun to air yet.

But after it launched, I went on *The View* to promote it. That's when people began to come up to me and say, "Oh my God, you're that guy from *All My Children*!"

People were fans, which was pretty cool.

"I love your story line," people would tell me.

"I love what you're about." It was always women, usually older women.

One friend told me, "You're going to get any cougar you want!"

I thought, *That's nice, but I don't want a cougar.* I told Dan about this newfound fact.

"Hey, cougars are my demographic. You better hook me up!" he joked.

In the meantime, I wondered how I could give the producers ideas to extend my storyline. I was scheduled to speak at a conference in Orlando in December, so I suggested to Julie that we shoot a scene of me actually speaking. She agreed, which showed me that the producers valued my input.

I felt like what I was doing was badass, but I didn't have anyone to share it with. I didn't have any friends in Manhattan. I did have one friend who lived on Long Island whom I hung out with a couple of times, but he was older than me, with a couple of kids. I'd text random friends in Dalton or Texas to occupy myself.

But on the set, a lot of the cast and crew seemed to be invested in me. When I did something well onstage, people applauded. There's a lot of competition in any performance and not everyone's going to survive. But most people genuinely supported me, though there was one awkward incident.

My first partner on the show was an experienced actress who'd recently come to *All My Children* from another soap. She was an Emmy-nominated performer and I respected her work, but she was less than happy to be paired with me. I focused on the task at hand and tried to do the best I could. I asked her to give me feedback so that our scenes together could be powerful.

There was a lot of buildup between her character and mine, and several times we came close to kissing onstage. Finally it was time. I walked on set into her character's apartment. A fire burned in the fireplace. We were having an intimate dinner. I was nervous and I got giggly, like I was five years old. Following the script, we gazed into each other's eyes. I kept giggling. A big-ass laugh was building up inside me like a volcano.

"What the hell are you giggling about?" the actress hissed at me.

I struggled to stifle my laugh. We resumed the scene. *I'm going to try to hold this laugh inside of me,* I thought, *and when she puts her lips on mine, I'll put all my energy into this kiss.* That was a good plan—no one needed to tell me how to kiss a woman. So I lurched in and kissed her until the director called, "Okay, clear!"

The actress pulled back and yelled, "Oh my God, the rookie used his tongue!"

I was totally, completely embarrassed. No one had bothered to tell me it was different when you kiss a woman on camera. Lesson learned. And fortunately, I never had to be in the position to do a love scene with her again. Her part was written off the show by the end of the year, and it was rumored that I might be paired next with Shannon Kane, a beautiful and freethinking actress. The story line revolved around a dance marathon in Pine Valley to raise money for a charity.

Julie called me into her office. "Can you dance?" she asked me.

Yeah, I can dance.

"But can you really dance?" she persisted.

"I was out last night and the bar was having a Michael Jackson dance competition," I told her. "I won."

After Shannon and I began our scenes together, one of our costars approached me. "Hey," she said, "I'd like to talk to you. Here's my number. Call me when you get a chance."

Cool, I thought. *Maybe we're friends?* This actress was a diva, pretty full of herself, but she was very experienced and I wanted her approval. I called her from the back of a taxi on my way to the airport.

We weren't friends. "I see the way you play against Shannon on-screen, and you're acting like a boy, not like a man," she said.

I was playing it exactly like the producers had instructed me, and I told her that.

"Oh, I'm so sorry," she backpedaled. But it was bull. She made me feel like some kid. I got so upset that my eyes actually teared up.

Moments like this gave me real pause. *I don't like this shit,* I'd think. *Why am I doing this?* Then I'd shake it off, tell myself that I wasn't going to allow these people to intimidate me. I spent most of my time hanging out with the crew and Diana, because I could relate well to them.

Shannon and I competed in Pine Valley's dance marathon, emerging victorious. The script brought us from our first meeting to becoming friends to me getting a crush on her to us having sex. By the end, we were engaged. Shannon was so much better to work with than my original partner.

"Try it this way," she'd suggest, or "Did you ever think of doing it like that?" She was encouraging and helpful and it was great to work with her.

Despite my minor setbacks, my time on *All My Children* convinced me that I liked acting. I felt like I was getting pretty good at it and I started to believe it was my future. I developed a strong fan base. I began to get mail from people all over the world. I read every single fan letter and in return sent an autographed photo. I attended the fan events and people went nuts for me when I was introduced, which was surreal.

On the street, it was different. People didn't recognize me so much. But one incident sticks in my mind.

I was in the Bronx with a friend, waiting for a ride home. As we stood chatting on the sidewalk, we heard a woman's loud voice: "Brot, is that you, motherfucker?"

Frowning, I looked over. Three rough-looking women were gaping at me. They were crackheads or prostitutes or both, in their tube tops and Daisy Dukes.

They ran at me, hooting with joy, as I backed away.

"Shit, that is you, motherfucker!" one of them screamed into my face, her spit stippling the air around me. She put her hands on my shoulders and jumped up and down. Here's what went through my mind: *Being on TV should get me every chick out there, and this is what I got.*

They wanted photos. "Aw, shit, take a picture, bitch!" yelled one woman to her friend.

"Move, bitch, it's my turn!" shouted another.

Then they wanted a group shot. My bewildered friend agreed to take it. I was standing with the three women when, at the last second, just when the shutter clicked, one of them threw her leg up on top of my arm so it looked like I was holding up her leg with my hand. That was all I needed, for the studio to see a picture like this.

When I signed on with *All My Children*, I didn't know whether my stint would last past the three months. I signed a one-year contract, but every three months I had to renew it. After I'd been on a whole year, the original contract expired and I was told to contact an entertainment attorney to negotiate a new one. This was in mid-September 2009.

But the ensuing year would see the demise of several daytime shows—*Guiding Light* and *As the World Turns* among them—and my cast mates on *All My Children* were wondering if we'd be next.

In August 2009, in the middle of one of the dance scenes that Shannon and I were shooting, an intercom voice summoned every single person to the studio across the hall, where *The View* was taped. Everyone settled nervously into the audience seats, Shannon and I next to each other. The president of ABC Entertainment daytime TV addressed our huge group of actors, crew, production, and other staff. The first thing he said was, "Relax, guys, we're not being canceled."

We'd heard rumors that the show might be moved to Los Angeles, which wasn't a bad idea to me. In fact, for a long time I'd felt that L.A. was in my future. When I first learned of the *All My Children* opportunity, I'd been in L.A. When I found out I'd gotten the part, I'd been in L.A. In my mind, L.A. was my next stop.

I leaned into Shannon. "I bet I'm going to L.A.," I whispered to her. "I know I'm going."

The executive told us that in December, *All My Children* would be transferring production to Los Angeles as a cost-saving move. The announcement shocked many of the cast and crew, a lot of whom had strong roots in New York and couldn't leave their mortgages and their kids' schools. The executives told us they'd let us know in the next few weeks who would be sent west. My confidence kicked in to overdrive. But word was slow in coming, so I walked around in limbo for a long time.

About three months earlier, in May 2009, I'd met a guy who ran a speakers' bureau out of Connecticut. He had a full roster of speakers on just about every topic and booked them before audiences at colleges and universities, corporate meetings, and other large groups. We decided to work together.

Since the producers were busy trying to figure out the details and logistics of the show's move, I had no idea what my fate had in store. *Screw it,* I thought, *I need to move ahead with my life,* so I began to book presentation dates. I'd tell my story, explain how I'd kept my head up, and talk about maintaining a positive outlook no matter what life threw at you.

Then in September I finally got my answer from *All My Children*: I was going to L.A. I was in shock, especially since I knew that there were a handful of experienced actors who weren't being included in the move. I told Julie I'd focus on being the best actor I could be.

And I was more than a little pleased to learn that Diana would be going to L.A. as well. We coached each other through the whole move. When I went to California to scope out apartments, I'd text her when I saw a good one. By December we were both out there. It was great to have a friend in this new town.

I realized I should put more effort into my acting, though, and Julie recommended an acting coach. I signed up for his class and attended every Tuesday evening for a couple of hours. We students were instructed to print out the scripts of various films, then pick a scene and act it out with a partner. The lessons provided the opportunity to exercise different roles outside of *All My Children*, but besides that it didn't really do anything for me.

In November, shortly before the move to Los Angeles, I was invited to be the grand marshal of the San Antonio Veterans Day Parade. While I was there, I looked up a couple of my old friends, and one night we went to dinner. While waiting for our table, the three of us grabbed seats at the bar. I looked over at the door as two women walked in. I made eye contact with one—a medium-complected Hispanic—and she smiled at me. *She's beautiful,* I thought. As we were escorted to our table we passed by her. I said hello, but she only smiled back. A few minutes later our waitress brought a drink over to me. "It's from that girl," she said, pointing at the one I'd greeted. I went over to their table and asked if I could sit down, and they said yes. The girl's name was Liz. She was a twenty-one-year-old college student and an Air Force reservist.

So began my next relationship. I flew her up to New York to hang out for a weekend. I enjoyed her company but I didn't really think of it becoming anything because I was focusing on my move.

Once in California, Liz regularly came out from Texas to visit me. Our relationship was okay until, you guessed it, I caught her in a lie. Yeah, this seems to be a theme in my relationships. Frequently these "lies" were lies of omission, but they were always about other guys. I'm not talking about "You said you went to the grocery store at four but it was really at two," but more like "You never told me you were still seeing your ex-boyfriend."

I decided to break it off with her, but then I remembered what my mom had said about pushing people away. Liz and I discussed our issues and decided to try again. In the spring, she broached the idea of moving in with me in L.A. I had gotten myself a nice little two-bedroom apartment in Studio City. By May I'd agreed, though I wasn't completely comfortable with the idea. I felt like I was trying for something that just wasn't there.

Around this time I needed to have a surgery on

my right eyelid. My eye was drying out a lot and it was very irritating. I'd known this surgery was necessary, but I'd been putting it off. So in an effort to continue to tell the story of Brot and not miss any time off of work, I asked the producer if we might be able to write the surgery into the story line. To my surprise, she agreed. I thought it was kick-ass that they were willing to accommodate me in the name of entertainment and bring attention to the fact that wounded warriors often aren't a quick fix.

Over Memorial Day weekend I flew to San Antonio to help Liz load her car with her stuff and her two dogs to make the drive west. I still had a nagging feeling of doubt about our relationship, which I tried to stifle. I knew Liz was drawn in by my newfound celebrity, and part of me even felt like it might be her main reason for dating me. And that didn't feel right at all.

Liz was suspicious of my connection with Diana, too. "Diana's my friend," I'd explain to her, again and again. By the time Liz moved out to L.A., Diana and I were hanging out together all the time. We'd go to movies, parties, dinner, everything.

In July Liz went to a training session in Ohio for work. She was gone for two weeks. During that time Diana and I went to the movies. Diana told me she felt it was wrong to go together, just me and her, because I had a girlfriend.

"Don't sweat it," I told her. "It's not like we're doing anything crazy."

Near the end of the month I was in New York. Diana's birthday was coming up, so I flew back to Los Angeles so that I wouldn't miss her celebration. Within weeks, I had asked Liz to move out. She was very upset. My feelings were blunted because I'd never really invested in the relationship.

Meanwhile, I had a new and entirely unexpected love enter my life.

In August an organization had asked me to speak at an event to raise money for the Wounded Warrior Project, a nonprofit that helps injured veterans transition from military active duty to civilian life. They also asked me to assist with the auction that was scheduled for the event and invited me to a barbecue the night before at the home of one of the sponsors.

The sponsor mentioned that he was storing some of the auction items there at his house.

"Like what?" I asked.

A puppy—a Labrador retriever that could be trained to be a service dog to a veteran. They brought the dog out to show me.

He looked like a stuffed animal. He was the cutest thing ever, and I mean *ever*. I held him all evening. I decided to try for him at the auction. I made up my mind that I'd bid up to $1,500, and not a penny more. I know that is a lot of money for a dog, but I knew it would go to a good cause.

The next night I went to the event and got up onstage. I auctioned off a couple of items, and then I told the audience, "The next thing really hurts me to put up here for you all. It's a two-month-old Lab."

I held him up and the audience melted. People began to bid. I had a friend in the audience who was bidding for me, but the numbers quickly surpassed my limit and finally the contest came down to one guy and a couple. Each said they'd pay $2,500, for a total of $5,000 for the dog.

I was devastated. One of the winners stood, the puppy in her arms. "I'd like to say something," she announced. She made her way to the podium. "We love this cause and we love coming every year," she said, addressing the audience. "And we love this puppy, but unfortunately there's no room in our house for this cute little thing."

She walked across the stage and put the puppy in my arms. "We'd like to give this puppy to J.R.," she said.

I was completely surprised and so freaking happy. It was meant to be.

I went into fatherhood mode right away, albeit doggy fatherhood. The very next day I put the puppy into my backpack and took him to the *All My Children* set, where dogs weren't allowed. I smuggled him into my dressing room, and then

I went to see Diana. "Come into my dressing room," I told her. "Just come now. I want to show you something."

After a while she came and knocked on my door. I had the puppy hidden under a blanket and he popped out. She went crazy over him.

I named him Romeo and took him everywhere with me. I had a trainer come in a couple of times to help me with his house-training, but other than that I trained him on my own. He's so in tune to me that even if he's running toward another dog, he'll turn mid-stride if I call his name. He's an amazing dog. He was my little baby.

By September 2010, coming up on a year since we'd moved to L.A., Diana and I had begun to spend more and more time together. We did stuff that couples would do, without being a couple. The more we hung out, the more I realized how much I liked to be around her. In October I finally put a voice to it.

I'd asked her to watch the first game of the NBA season with me.

She said yes, but then she called to tell me that she couldn't get out of work in time.

I asked her to come by anyway, later.

She said no.

All of a sudden it came out: "Do you ever think of me differently?"

She hesitated. "What do you mean?"

"You know what I mean. More than a friend," I said.

She went right at it, trying to play it off like I was drunk and operating under liquid courage. But I wasn't.

"No," she said. "We're friends."

So we continued to see each other at work, and our relationship didn't change.

One night in November I asked her to be my guest at an event I was emceeing. She agreed and came over after work to change into her evening outfit. She put on her dress in my bathroom and then asked me to zip her up.

Hmm, that's what you do when you're in a relationship, I thought. Later, on the way home from the event, I put my hand on hers in the car. She ignored the move and kept on talking. *Forget it,* I thought. *I'm done with this.*

Still, we maintained our connection as friends. At Thanksgiving, I went home to Dalton and Diana went home to New York. We talked for hours every night. We burned up the phone lines like we were teenagers, talking about anything and everything.

Finally, when we both returned to California, we got together to discuss our relationship in person, and that was our beginning.

They say that opposites attract, and maybe that's the case with Diana and me. Diana's upbringing, for example, could not have been any more different from mine. She grew up surrounded by family. Her mother and her biological dad divorced when she was two, but her dad stayed in her life for some years after. Her mom and stepfather got together when Diana was five, so she was always raised by two parents and had a boatload of grandparents. She was an only child until age nine. She never saw her parents fight; it's not that they didn't, but they didn't do it in front of Diana and her two younger sisters.

Diana's mom put her into every activity she wanted to be in and even those she didn't know she wanted to be in: ballet, gymnastics, track, basketball. She lived in the same neighborhood—Sunnyside, Queens—her entire life and went to Catholic schools. Although her family wasn't rich, by her own admission her parents gave her everything she wanted or needed—a Sweet Sixteen party, money to go out with her friends, a car when she was seventeen, a basketball hoop in front of the house, a home where her friends were always welcome to hang out. She was a cheerleader at Christ the King High School, in her sweater and turtleneck vest; short pleated white, red, and gold skirt; and Nike sneakers—belly always covered. She also ran track and cross-country and played basketball. Her parents insisted that Diana get good grades, and she delivered. She was the salutatorian of her eighth grade class, an honors student, and went to college on a partial academic scholarship.

But we had one major thing in common: We enjoyed being with each other. For Valentine's Day, she gave me a cooking class we'd do together. I surprised her with a trip to Northern California. There, standing on the Golden Gate Bridge—amid our visits to wineries, to Alcatraz, to romantic restaurants—this amazing feeling came over me when I realized that I loved this girl.

I decided to ratchet down my speaking schedule, stay home more, and enjoy my life and enjoy being with Diana. It was so natural with her. We were moving fast, but we'd known each other for a couple of years already. It's normal to be on a high when you first start a relationship, but this was more. She was solid and trustworthy. We had the same sense of humor and laughed together all the time. She was feisty and self-reliant—although I was, too, so sometimes we butted heads. We finished each other's sentences and knew what the other was thinking. I'd say something and she'd exclaim, "Oh my God, I was just thinking about that! God strike me down right now!"

"God is tired of hearing that. That's like trying to name-drop—it's not cool," I'd reply.

I told my mom that one thing I really appreciated about Diana was that she didn't give off a flirtatious vibe to other guys. To me, she's affectionate and loving, but I didn't have to worry about her when I wasn't around. If a dude is going to go after her, it would be because he wanted to, not because she was inviting it. With this reassurance, even with my track record with women, I let my defenses fall away.

Meanwhile, Tinseltown wasn't finished with the surprises for me. I began to hear buzz on social media and at fan events that I'd be a good candidate for an ABC show called *Dancing with the Stars*. I didn't think much about it until April, when the *All My Children* executives called everyone into the studio and told us the show had been canceled. Taping would cease in August 2011.

Many of the cast and crew were upset that they'd picked up and moved across the country for a show that had ended little more than a year later. I didn't blame them, but my situation was different: I hadn't disrupted a family, and the move had put me smack into the middle of the entertainment industry, just where I thought I wanted to be. The *All My Children* casting director helped me to assemble a package and reels so I could look around for an agent to represent me. I wanted to continue acting. And now that I had my companion, I felt I could focus on this other aspect of my life.

Right after the *All My Children* announcement went public, I received a text from a friend back in Dalton. "What about *Dancing with the Stars*?"

Hmm, I thought. For the first time, I actually considered it. I went into Julie's office one day and asked her opinion. She said she thought it was a great idea and that I should pursue it. Two *All My Children* actors—Susan Lucci and Cameron Mathison—had been competitors on the show in earlier seasons. Julie said she'd put in a call to a *Dancing with the Stars* contact.

A few weeks later my phone rang. It was May 2011, just after the eighth anniversary of my accident. The *Dancing with the Stars* casting director was on the other end of the line. We set up a meeting for an upcoming Friday in June. On that day, the casting director and another executive questioned me about my background. They asked me to tell them how much I enjoyed dancing, if I'd ever had formal dance instruction, and whether I was healthy enough to compete. By this time I was finished with my surgeries—my hands had straightened out and my grafts had healed. I was in good shape.

"The show is physically demanding," the casting director said. "Do you think you can do it?"

You know my answer.

They told me they'd decide the cast within the next couple of weeks.

More than a month later the casting director emailed me, but she didn't have a decision yet. I really had to know soon because I needed to book my future speaking engagements.

The wait dragged on, day after day, week after week, until one day in August she texted me to say that she'd be calling me in a couple of hours to make me an official offer. I was excited beyond words. At the same time, I was emotional because I knew this opportunity would change my life, exposing me to an even larger national audience. Diana and I hugged each other for the longest time. Neither of us could believe it.

I was invited to meet my dancing partner at the end of August. No one had given me any clue about who it would be. I was incredibly nervous, like a schoolkid going to pick up his date before the prom.

I waited outside the meeting room, and a producer came over to me. He explained how the meeting would go down.

"When you walk in, be sure to close the door behind you," he said. "Then walk over to her and greet her. Once we do it we may have to reenact it from a different angle."

At their signal, I opened the door and my eyes landed on Karina Smirnoff. Of course I knew who she was, an amazing Ukrainian-born dancer who'd appeared in nine seasons of the show.

I was stoked and gave her a big hug. She's a sweet and passionate person and we clicked from the very first moment. She hadn't heard of me beforehand; she said they'd pulled her aside while she was waiting to meet me and told her that she'd be dancing with a war veteran.

"I have a special place in my heart for the military and their families," she said, "but I was a little concerned. Like, what war? Was this going to be an elderly veteran?"

She was super-excited, she said, and told me that six months earlier she'd actually pitched a show—slugged "Dancing with the Heroes"—to the network. They'd passed on it but now she got to dance with me, which was the basis for her pitch anyway. She told me that *Dancing with the Stars* is the coolest thing she's ever done, and that it gives her a high similar to traditional competition.

We said a lot to each other that first morning, just sitting and talking together for hours about some really personal stuff. It was a big heart-to-heart. We both loved performing and sharing what we love the most with other people. We didn't want to just entertain; we wanted to bring the audience into our world.

Dancing with the Stars is "very emotionally fulfilling," she told me. "You find levels of feeling that you didn't think were there. It teaches you about yourself and how to handle certain situations."

Karina described the intensity of the *Dancing with the Stars* experience, both for the celebrity and the professional. "Every week the dances become like your little babies," she said. "Nothing can prepare you for this. If we go all the way, it's an insanely grueling schedule. Even your hair follicles will be exhausted. You'll wake up beat, and you still have a whole day ahead of you."

I wasn't afraid of hard work and, luckily, I wasn't experiencing any residual effects of my injuries that might handicap my development as a dancer. Even so, I certainly knew it was going to be difficult. That's all I heard from the professionals, the producers, and the former contestants. I felt optimistic about my run, because I'd always been a good dancer with easy rhythm. One of the first questions from Karina to me that first day was: Can you dance?

I went to the safest and goofiest move I had—the running man, which I followed with a skillful sprinkler move. She laughed. I felt ridiculous.

"I can't dance on the spot with no music!" I said. "Where's my music?"

She said our music for the first week would be for a Viennese waltz.

"A Vietnam what?" I asked.

Karina laughed again, but I honestly didn't have any idea what that was. She showed me a move where I had to spread out my arms like a swan. Then she put me into this hold as if I were clasping a box. Then I had to twirl around with my arms lifted and my shoulders down.

I never regretted signing up, but during those first few hours I wondered what in the hell I'd gotten myself into.

We started to sway around the room, but the pace was too fast for me. We stopped a few times to start all over. The great thing about the three weeks leading up to the first show was that we were only supposed to rehearse up to five hours per day. The producers didn't want anyone to get hurt prior to the premiere by pushing themselves too hard. Although five hours were more than I'd ever done, it wasn't as bad as I thought it would be.

We had about four days of rehearsal before the official announcement of the cast. On the big day, Diana and I were picked up at my apartment by a town car and driven to the CBS studios in Holly-wood. Everything was a big secret. We pulled into the drop-off area where they'd erected a tent to cover the entrance so that no paparazzo would be able to see us. I thought it was pretty crazy that the cameras would even care about little ole me.

We walked in and I was taken to a holding area where the cast was sitting, waiting to be briefed about the forthcoming live telecast announcement. We were going to have a dress rehearsal before the live shot.

I introduced myself to Los Angeles Lakers player Ron Artest (who would soon change his name to Metta World Peace) and sat next to him. I thought about how cool it was that I'd watched him play basketball so many times, and now we were sitting together, chatting. I looked over and saw Ricki Lake and flashed to watching her talk show when I was growing up. Then Nancy Grace walked in. I leaned over to Ron and said, "Dude, Nancy Grace just walked in."

I figured that since I'd whispered this to him and we were in the middle of a briefing he'd keep his mouth closed. But nope, not Ron.

He looked up. "Nancy Grace, everyone!" he shouted.

She smiled.

Learning the Viennese waltz was hard because Karina put a move in the routine that was like a trick. I was supposed to swing her around on the floor by her hands. Every time we tried to do it, I'd either fall or both of us would tumble down.

After a couple of weeks, Karina called me one morning on the way to rehearsal. "I think we should take out that element and do something else," she said. I was getting worried about injuring her, so I agreed.

At the studio we performed the routine for one of the producers, who persuaded us to leave in the tricky element. "That's the greatness of this show," he told us. "You can pull it off."

We decided to keep the element and continued to work on it. Pro dancer and cast member Mark Ballas gave me a couple of tips. We danced the routine in front of several of the other cast members, including reality-show player Kristin

Cavallari, singer Chynna Phillips, and soccer star Hope Solo. It was the first time any of us had seen anyone else in the group dance.

I felt so confident that I yelled out "booya!" during the middle of the routine.

"What the hell was that about?" Karina asked.

I told her that I felt good and a "booya" was the appropriate way to express that.

She laughed and said she understood.

When it came time to work on our second week's routine, the jive, Karina was like a child who loves to show off to her parents. Every time someone would come into our studio, she would offer to dance our routine for them. I was nervous about this, but when we'd finish, people always seemed excited.

"You guys are going to win this!"

Of course we loved to hear this, but we always played it down and stayed focused.

Every single dance offered a different degree of difficulty. The jive was a fast dance for which I had to learn to kick properly and keep up the pace.

The night of the premiere we were called out to dance. We stood in our positions, waiting for the start cue. I looked over at Karina and nodded my head, telling her without words that I was ready. Our eyes locked and she smiled at me, and in the next moment the announcer introduced us. Over the weeks, we found our connection was so strong that we didn't need words to express it. In the middle of the competition our hearts were beating hard with nerves and excitement, but it seemed like they beat at the same time.

The week-three dance was to be the rumba and represent the celebrities' most memorable year. For me, that was 2003, the year I was injured. Karina and I decided to dedicate our dance to our military—specifically, to all those men and women who didn't make it back home from war. Karina emphasized that this needed to be so much more than a dance; it needed to be a musical, a performance.

This homage added to the already intense pressure and marked the first time that Karina and I butted heads. On the Sunday before show day, we were practicing our routine and making touch-ups. I told her that I wasn't happy with the routine and that I didn't look good dancing it. I wanted the dance to be perfect, since it was a tribute.

Karina reminded me that she was the pro and would decide whether our dance was up to par.

"You don't know what you're talking about," I said.

Karina turned around and walked out without a word.

I stood stock-still after she left.

"Are you okay?" asked a crew member.

"Yeah," I said.

"Go home and relax," he said. "Rest a bit and everything will work out."

I took his advice. The following day—show day—I found Karina in the studio and apologized. I told her why I'd acted the way I had. She said she understood and assured me that I'd go out there and do a great job.

Right before our introduction later that day, they aired the package they'd put together about my background and our past week in rehearsal. All day we'd remained unemotional, and we'd both been worried that we wouldn't be able to achieve the focus that would take our performance from great to out of this world.

"I know I'm asking a lot," Karina said, "but I need you to go to that place one more time, and I need you to take me with you."

I have no memory of the performance because I was crying so hard.

When we finished, Karina and I gathered ourselves to soak in the feedback from the audience. They gave us a standing ovation.

"Tonight you did something extraordinary," judge Carrie Ann Inaba told us, calling our performance "one of the most profound, honest dances."

Judge Bruno Tonioli crowed at us. "You danced from your heart," he said. "I could feel every emotion. It was a great, great achievement."

Our routines got stronger and more personal

each week. We always joined hands and said a prayer before performing.

Week six really tested our partnership. The required dance was the quickstep, which to me was the most difficult because I had to keep my arms raised as I moved my feet with lightning speed. Karina and I usually had our routines down cold by Friday or Saturday morning at the latest, then we'd spend Saturday and Sunday refining our steps. This week was different. By ten o'clock Saturday night, I was still having problems with the routine and we were getting snippy with each other. Even though she was right, I was fed up with her telling me I was wrong. I was just plain tired of doing the routine. I kept stepping on Karina's toes, and I was having a hard time keeping up the pace. Karina would become frustrated and push me off and stop. I'd go back to the starting position and say, "Let's do it again," and off we'd go.

It was a struggle, but we finally got it down. Who would've dreamed that dance would get us two tens and a nine, our highest scores since the competition started.

Meanwhile, behind the scenes, whenever we had a little downtime—and there was very little downtime—I got to spend time with my castmates. I found myself talking to Rob Kardashian a lot and joking around with him. I'm definitely not a Kardashian fan, but I came to see Rob as a pretty chill dude over the course of the season. We hung out a fair bit, and I pulled a few pranks on him, like busting in on his rehearsals or interviews. He did the same thing to me and Karina. A couple of times I played silly jokes on him, hiding his shoes or his phone. Sometimes he'd come into our studio and turn off the lights before slamming the door. One time his partner, Cheryl Burke, left her dancing shoes in the studio. I put plastic spiders inside them and stuck them on top of the fence at the entrance to the building. The next day she came into our room laughing and told me she was going to kick my butt.

I spent some time talking with Chaz Bono about his upcoming book and his speaking engagements. The only child of Sonny Bono and Cher, Chaz had recently undergone gender reassignment. He was cool and didn't seem to care if people might be judging him.

Ricki wasn't as welcoming as she might be under different circumstances. I think the pressure got to her, and she was very competitive, which was great for the show but not so good for camaraderie.

Hope would say, "I'm not used to this world, and you guys are." The show really took her outside her comfort zone. I was sensitive to that because I was fairly new to entertainment as well, so I spent time urging her to just relax. Her partner was Maks Chmerkovskiy, and Karina and he had a history and they didn't talk or get along at all. Hope and I didn't want their relationship to define ours, although it was the basis for some awkward-ness.

When it came down to it, I liked everyone in the cast. David Arquette and I had a few good conversations about agents. Nancy and I had Chick-fil-A in common—it's my favorite fast food and the company originated in Georgia, where Nancy's from. (Sometimes you have to dig deep to find that unifying element.)

My relationship with Karina was on a whole different level. I think we'll be friends for the rest of our lives. And we learned that even if you love your partner, there are days you just don't want to see each other. The way they eat or talk or take a breath can be annoying. We had that moment right before week nine. The way I walked pissed her off, and her hair pissed me off. Sometimes we'd tell each other that we were sick of each other, and then we'd say, "Okay, that felt great. Want to get a snack?"

Other days I simply felt like seeing how far I could push my partner. I'd come into rehearsal and just start pressing her buttons. I'd try to turn dance details into a major motion picture, which would completely aggravate her. To keep me in line, she'd make deals with me.

"You need to help me or I'm not going to help you," she'd say. "If you give me two hours of really trying, we'll dork around afterward."

During week nine, I was complaining in rehearsal because the Latin heels were killing my feet. I wanted to wear rubber-soled shoes. Karina warned me against it but finally relented.

"You can wear them just this once."

So the one and only time I wore sneakers, I twisted my ankle and we hit the floor hard.

Karina said, "Okay, maybe we should try that again."

But I was still lying there, in pain.

Ankles aren't going to kill you, but when you have a sprain it hurts like crazy. Besides, this was the same ankle I'd injured playing football in high school. Karina asked the doc to shoot my ankle with cortisone to take away the pain. "We'll wrap it as tight as we can to give it support."

No way, no injections, I told her. I thought I could work through the pain.

The Argentine tango we were doing had all the elements for a perfect score. I managed to complete all the lifts, but I couldn't put all my weight on the ankle. The next thing I know, I was stomping my foot and saying the f-word on camera.

Karina wanted to slap me. That dance earned us our lowest scores since week two of the competition.

During the week of our final dance, our free-style, we were both nursing injuries. Karina had strained her neck and I was still favoring my ankle. By our dress rehearsal, Karina's confidence had hit an all-time low. All week we'd been screwing up our lifts, and she was freaking out.

But once we landed the first lift in our final dance, we knew we were on the bullet train to the finish line. It gave us the energy to go all the way through.

Making it to the finale was fantastic for me. If I won, it would be a major accomplishment. In the last minutes, we were standing there with the other finalists, Rob and Cheryl, waiting to learn the verdict.

Host Tom Bergeron paused, each passing moment making a loud ticking noise in my brain.

I looked at Karina and muttered to her, "Will they just tell us already?"

She bit her lip.

Then Tom said our names. We literally jumped for joy. I was especially thrilled that I'd been able to help Karina win her first competition after so many years on the show. Tom handed me the disco ball trophy and I held it up high. That thing weighs a ton! The whole cast ran out onto the floor. Dance pro Derek Hough hoisted me up on his shoulders. I struggled to balance, momentarily worried that I'd drop the trophy on someone's head.

He released me and I felt someone tugging on

my shirt. I looked down into my mom's proud face. I put my arm around her and pulled her close. To think that eight years earlier I'd been leaning on my mom, trying to learn to walk again. Now I was a ballroom dancing champion. What a journey.

CHAPTER FOURTEEN

Full of Heart

Right after the credits finished rolling, Karina and I were herded off the stage into a back room where we appeared via satellite on the late-night talk show *Jimmy Kimmel Live*.

"Purple heart, schmurple heart," Jimmy said, "you got a mirror ball!"

From there we were taken back out to the floor, where we had a minute with every press outlet gathered. And from there, all three finalist couples said goodbye to most of our special guests and were driven to the Burbank airport. With Karina's mom and my mom, we boarded a jet and flew overnight to New York.

In the morning we were at the *Good Morning America* studios, where we danced, and then it was on to *The View*, where we danced again. I was completely exhausted. My cheeks hurt from smiling so much. My phone blew up from all the emails, texts, and voice mails I was getting from family, friends, and people I'd met over the years.

After this three-month dancing boot camp,

from August through November, the world had become surreal. Everywhere I went, everyone wanted to take a photo of me. I was on a cloud, but it wasn't cloud nine. Don't get me wrong, I was overjoyed, but I felt like I just wanted to sit down for six months and let my mind and body catch up and relax.

What my fellow cast members and viewers didn't know was that I had been dealing with some developments in my personal life the last weeks of the show.

Diana and I had been a couple for nearly a year now. Everything was so natural with her and it felt right to spend all our time together. When I wasn't working, that is.

Ever since Diana and I had made the transition from friends to more-than-friends, I'd supported her crazy hours at work. I brought her coffee or lunch, put gas in her car if she didn't have time to do it herself, or just stepped up in whatever way I could. Other than that, all she ever saw me do was take Romeo to the park.

Once I began rehearsals for *Dancing*, everything changed. I became really focused on my career. Not only was I crazy busy, but I was obsessing about my professional future. I was determined to make the most of the opportunity.

On September 8 I had arrived home from rehearsal to the apartment we now shared and jumped into the shower. We were going to meet some friends for the kickoff of the NFL season: the Green Bay Packers versus the New Orleans Saints.

I was sitting on the floor putting on my shoes when Diana walked into the room and closed the door behind her. She sat down on the bed and listened to me talk about my day and the steps Karina had taught me. Finally I paused to look at her.

"What's up?" I asked. She had a strange expression on her face. It made me feel nervous.

She hesitated a second. "You know how I've been feeling a little weird lately?" she began.

I nodded.

"I took a pregnancy test." She didn't need to finish, but she did: "I'm pregnant."

I jumped up to take her in my arms.

"Are you cool with it?" she asked.

"This is amazing," I replied. It *was* amazing.

Then the real world crept back in. I sank down on the bed and thought about how a baby wasn't part of our plan. Things were just kicking off for me, and I hoped they would continue to. I thought about how I wasn't necessarily ready for this yet, that the timing wasn't right. I'd always wanted to be a father, but now?

Diana needed me to tell her that everything was going to be okay, but I didn't. Because I didn't know if it would be okay.

In the coming days, I found myself withdrawing

from her, mulling over the prospect of father-hood. I knew I'd have a crazy schedule after we wrapped the show—how would that dovetail with the birth of a baby? And what about me and Diana? When would we have time to enjoy each other as a couple?

To be fair, Diana was reflecting on the preg-nancy, too. We agreed to keep the news to our-selves for now.

I tried to keep the thoughts of a baby from distracting me as I practiced with Karina, but she knew something was up, and I finally shared the news with her.

The demands of the show seemed to seep over into everyone's relationships at home—that's just the way it was. It wasn't Karina herself who bugged Diana, it was all the time I spent with Karina practicing, day in and day out. My relation-ship with Diana was complicated further by the weight of an unplanned pregnancy.

Before the premiere of *Dancing with the Stars*, I had to fulfill a couple of speaking commitments in other cities. Karina came with me so we wouldn't lose any practice time. I invited Diana to accompany us on one of the trips. The two women hung out together and got along just fine, which went a long way toward alleviating any mis-givings Diana may have had.

When we told Diana's parents about the pregnancy, they digested the news slowly. Her parents are very traditional—marriage, then baby—so their enthusiasm was tempered by the fact that their daughter and I weren't married. They also worried that we were rushing our relationship.

Diana began to feel like she was figuring everything out on her own. She was excited and wanted me to be at the same place she was. There were a lot of nights when I'd come home from rehearsal and we'd hash it out. Eventually I realized I just needed time to process our new reality.

After about a month, I was ready: Okay, this is happening. We embraced it.

After Karina and I won *Dancing with the Stars*, Diana and I took a little vacation to the Cayman Islands, our "babymoon," as she called it. We were so ready to get away from it all and have a little downtime. I was looking forward to being one of the masses instead of a celebrity. I figured no one would care about us outside the United States. Not so.

The fans were out in full force—at the airport, inside the grocery store, in the streets, on the beach.

"We loved you on *Dancing with the Stars*!" they'd yell.

"The whole island watches!" they'd shout. People approached us, took photos on their cell phones. Even the other tourists were agog.

But we managed to put a wall of privacy around

us and enjoy our time together, lying on the beach and playing around in the water.

On our return to L.A. we found ourselves dodging paparazzi at the airport. The next morning I was still asleep in my bed when I heard Diana squawk: "What? Wait! Oh my God!"

She was looking at her phone. "There are photos of us on the beach in the Cayman Islands in the tabloids!"

We'd had no idea people were photographing us during our more private times. It hit me at that moment: I was a celebrity now. In a way it was cool, but all sense of privacy was out the door. My life was never going to be the same, at least for the foreseeable future. I'd have to conduct myself with care.

One thing I understand about my fans is that they feel like they have been part of my journey —the people who watched me on *All My Children* were with me from the start, and those who tuned in every Monday and Tuesday to *Dancing with the Stars* saw me grow and helped me win. I'm not untouchable—I'm one of them. It's because of my background, my blue-collar family, my military service.

I'm so grateful to have had the opportunities I've had and the perks that come along with them. For example, in 2012 I was lucky enough to attend Super Bowl XLVI in Indianapolis, where the New England Patriots faced the New York Giants. There I saw pro athletes, such as Deion Sanders, whom I revered when I was growing up. I loved the Dallas Cowboys and was thrilled at the sight of him playing on my TV every week. At the Super Bowl, some guests were invited to play a game of flag football with various celebrities and former NFL players. One of my teammates was Sanders.

And although I was just out there having fun, something really good happened on the field that day. I met former player Martin Gramatica, who does construction now. I introduced him to Dan, and Martin's company partnered with Operation Finally Home to build a house for a wounded veteran in Tampa.

How do you process this kind of life? I can understand now why a lot of celebrities get nutty. One minute you're hanging out with your old friends and the next you're playing football with your childhood idols.

In October 2011 I was on the cover of *People*. It's hard to explain how surreal it was to see my face smiling out at me—and everyone else— while waiting in the checkout line at the drug-store or picking up milk at the market. The very next month I was named as an honoree in the magazine's annual feature, "Sexiest Man Alive." This distinction triggered a wave of emotions in me. I reflected on the way I'd frequently viewed myself during the previous eight years—as someone whose scars defined him. To me, this magazine credit meant I'd grabbed the big win on behalf of everyone out there who has disfigurements, disabilities, or insecurities, showing the world a different kind of sexy.

Sometimes the fame can have a downside, like when an overzealous fan wrote inappropriate comments on social media about Diana. I may be fair game, but my loved ones are off-limits.

But then, most of us are susceptible to getting a little kooky over celebrities. Diana and I attended the Screen Actors Guild Awards in Los Angeles, which was a big show, red carpet and all. At the after-party, I almost bumped into comedienne and actress Tina Fey. I don't have a thing for her, but I think she's mad hilarious. But suddenly, standing there, I was so nervous I couldn't even say hi. I instantly developed a crush on her.

All night long, I was saying to Diana, "Let's go walk by Tina Fey again." I was goo-goo about her. "I want to make out with Tina Fey."

"Go ahead," Diana said. "I'll bet you can't even talk to her."

I never did.

Still, I wouldn't trade my fame for the world— the good outweighs the bad, particularly when I get to use it for the right reasons. I don't mean when Diana and I go out to dinner at a popular restau-rant and get escorted to the front of the line. That's nice for us, but shitty for everyone else. No, for me, it's about the platform that allows me to bring attention to something important—especially my favorite cause. It's icing on the cake when something funny happens in conjunc-tion.

In April 2012 I made it to the White House. The visit was in observance of the "Joining Forces" initiative to honor and support veterans and military families. I'd been asked to serve as a judge on a panel to determine grants for various veterans' organizations. I'd be meeting the First Lady, Michelle Obama, and the Second Lady, Jill Biden. It was a crazy privilege, and I was so excited.

Once I was admitted onto the grounds, I saw this guy Steve I know. He is the president of a veterans' organization and, I have to admit, someone I've always wanted to impress. We began to talk and soon were ushered into the Diplomatic Reception Room, where we'd pose for photos with Mrs. Obama and Mrs. Biden.

"I'm going to go to the restroom," Steve said.

"Do you know how to find it?" a White House attendant asked.

"Yes, I know exactly where it is."

Wow, I thought, he knows exactly how to get to

the closest restroom in the White House. He's really a heavy hitter.

"I have to go, too," I said, so we walked together to the men's room, chatting. The two urinals were a bit too close together for my comfort, so I headed into the stall and closed the door. We continued to shoot the breeze. I unzipped my fly and tried to do my business. To put it politely, for some reason I was only able to expel the smallest amount. In the now quiet of the restroom, all sounds were magnified. Oh Lord, I thought. I'm stuck here. Now Steve is going to think I wanted to come to the bathroom just to hang out with him.

I closed my zipper and went to flush the toilet. I saw a little dial on the side of it. This was the White House—maybe it was a fancy way to flush the toilet. I reached down and turned it a little. I was appalled to see a stream of water shoot straight up at me, soaking my crotch before I could dodge. It was the bidet.

I heard Steve announce that he was finished. I walked out of the stall and washed my hands, trying to look natural, as if I didn't have a big wet spot on the front of my pants. If I were able to blush, my face would've been flame red. Steve and I walked back to the Diplomatic Reception Room. I didn't look down. The aides told me that I'd be the first one to pose with Mrs. Obama and Mrs. Biden. When I finally received a copy of the photo in the mail, I was amused to see that the image showed all of us only from the waist up.

January 1, 2012. I'd been asked to serve as the grand marshal of the Pasadena Tournament of Roses, the parade that precedes the annual Rose Bowl football game.

Everything was over the top. They gave us a luxurious two-story suite. My mother and Diana's parents were flown in first class. I received a hero's welcome as I rode in a convertible along the parade route. It was the perfect beginning to an exciting year, and we were on the highest of highs.

But at the end of the trip, while Diana's parents were still in town, we learned that her seventeen-year-old sister, Lauren, who lived with her parents in Queens, had unexpectedly passed away.

It was another cold reminder to me that nothing is forever. As great as the first-class treatment can be, it doesn't bring back Lauren. This was the worst reality check anyone could ever receive. And it made me appreciate my mom even more, how she'd never gotten the chance to say goodbye to Anabel, the same way Diana's parents hadn't been able to say goodbye to their daughter.

Diana was devastated by her little sister's death. She began to look upon her pregnancy almost as a sign. While she didn't believe that God takes a life to give a life, she felt that God knew he was going to take Lauren from us—and so this new baby would be a gift. Not to replace, but to ease the pain.

And she has. On May 2, 2012, Lauryn Anabelle was born. Anyone who's a parent knows that the emotion surrounding the birth of a child is impossible to put into words. Fatherhood is something I've always wanted. But after I got injured, I thought it would never happen for me.

When I was a kid and that third Sunday in June rolled around, I always wished my mother, "Happy Father's Day, too, Mom." Now I just want her to be able to enjoy the rest of her life and do what she wants to do, instead of what she has to do. I want her to have fun with her granddaughter and be able to come spend time with Belle whenever she wants. After eleven years, my mom's relationship with Celestino has ended, and she's thinking about what she wants to do next.

As excited as I am when I behold my tiny daughter, there's a lot of fear in me as well. I hope I do everything right with her, whether it's changing her diaper today, fixing a scraped knee when she falls off her first bike, or helping mend a broken heart when some guy she's dating does her wrong.

But the most important thing is that she'll always know that her dad is there for her. The best part for me will be witnessing all she becomes and grows into. From her first steps to her first report card to walking her down the aisle, I'm excited about all of it.

One thing about being in the spotlight is having people come up to me because they've heard my story or read an article about me or watched me on television. Almost invariably, they say, "I don't think I could've gone through that at age nineteen."

And almost invariably, I say, "With all due respect, what makes you think *I* was ready to go through that?"

The truth is, no nineteen-year-old could imagine living through such an event. I don't think any forty-five-year-old could.

What I've learned in my life, and one of the reasons I decided to write this book, is that people need to understand and accept that everything we go through in life will prepare us for our own big explosion. In my case, it was an actual blast, but for others it could be a painful divorce, illness, job loss. No matter what, we are all going to face the unexpected (and the unwanted) challenges in our lives, and what matters is the way we cope.

Back in 2004, when I first saw my old pals from my unit and I was so angry and hurt that they'd basically ignored me, I didn't understand what that explosion had meant to *them*. I began to feel differently in 2010 when I started to work on this book and I reached out to some of the guys to get their version of events. Hearing them talk about that day in Iraq made me realize that a lot of them hadn't reached out to me because they didn't know what to say. Even years later, some still felt guilty, wondering if they could have done anything differently to protect their men.

I'm very grateful when people share their stories with me, when they tell me that something I've said has resonated with or inspired them. And if there is a silver lining to my experience, it is that—the chance to show others that even during the worst of times, we can still maintain hope.

One woman, a cancer survivor, told me that she never left the house without a wig, because she had lost all her hair from chemotherapy and felt embarrassed about the way she looked. She said that after meeting me, she went out minus her wig, and for the first time since her illness she felt proud of who she is.

In 2011 I traveled to a high school in Los Angeles for a speaking engagement. Later in the day, I was able to meet with some of the kids, mostly members of the school's theater group. One girl, a brunette with dark skin, started crying when I hugged her. I didn't ask her for an explanation; I just held her. Then I stepped back and gripped both of her shoulders with my hands. "Whatever you're going through—it will get better," I told her. I hoped that it would.

Later that year, when I was a contestant on *Dancing with the Stars*, I received a letter from this student, addressed to me care of the ABC offices in L.A. "Dear J.R.," it read. "I just wanted to tell you that meeting you saved my life." She wrote that she had cried in my arms that day because she had been at a low point. She had surrendered her life in her mind, and she had already figured out how, when, and where she'd reach this sad goal. But after hearing me speak, she'd put her plans on hold. Watching me battle week after week on *Dancing* had prompted her to rethink her own challenges. How awesome is that?

Of course, I share a particularly vital bond with burn survivors. We're tough people, and nobody in the world knows pain the way we do. Fortunately for me, I was able to meet one remarkable teen who inspires me as much as she says I inspire her. Her name is Jenna Bullen, and at age three she was burned over 95 percent of her body when a water heater ignited in her family garage. Jenna's goal is to become a motivational speaker.

In 2011 Jenna, who is from Oklahoma City, was a guest on Dr. Drew's show *Lifechangers*. The producers had heard that Jenna was a fan of mine, so they had me tape a greeting to her that she viewed in front of the studio audience. What she didn't know is that they'd invited me to the studio to surprise her that day. It was a magic moment when I came up behind the unsuspecting girl onstage to give her a big hug.

After that, Jenna became my lucky charm. She came to Los Angeles to be my special guest in the audience of *Dancing with the Stars*. She helped me pay it forward when we produced a public service announcement together benefiting the Phoenix Society for Burn Survivors. Our aim was to get the word out about the resources and network of support for others like us.

In 2009 I met Army Sergeant Joel Tavera, one of the thousands of service men and women who have been injured since the wars in Afghanistan and Iraq began. Joel's life-changing event occurred in March 2008, when a rocket blast burned more than 60 percent of his body, destroyed his right leg, disordered his brain, and caused him to have four fingers amputated. It also left him blind.

I met Joel during one of my trips to BAMC to visit troops. I immediately fell in love with his attitude, his sense of humor, his outlook for the future, and his plans to give back to others. I promised his family that I'd follow him every-where he goes, and I have. Joel and I have become great friends and talk about everything from recovery to life opportunities to our old days in the Army. In between visits, we text like a couple of teenagers. Joel is another person who gives me as much as I give him.

I increasingly think that housekeeper in the ICU was right when she said that someday I would find out why this accident happened to me—perhaps no time more so than one night in the fall of 2010. I'd hopped into my truck with Romeo, who goes practically everywhere with me, and gone to get something to eat. I'd just gotten back into town and was exhausted. I was really looking forward to relaxing in front of *Monday Night Football*.

I stopped for gas on the way home and, while I was filling my tank, Romeo somehow leaned against the lock on the inside of the truck door. With a click, he'd locked me out. I didn't realize it until I tried to get back in.

"Oh no!" I wailed.

I peered through the glass and there, on the console, were my keys and my phone. I spent a few fruitless minutes trying to sweet-talk Romeo into unlocking the door—yeah, I know, but I was desperate. None of my loud baby-voice entreaties of "Come here, buddy!" caused him to miraculously develop language skills. He wagged his tail furiously and barked, but he wasn't able to make the connection.

Thanking the skies for small favors that I still had my wallet, I went into the shop and bought some Doritos and a Gatorade and asked for my change in quarters for the pay phone. I borrowed the phone book and looked up locksmiths. The first two I called told me it would be at least an hour-and-a-half wait. The third one said he could be right over.

A few blessed minutes later, this skinny Latino guy, with the drained look of a person who's been working too much for not enough pay, showed up. But he took on a new energy once he realized that he knew me from *All My Children*, and we got to talking. He told me he and his wife were having issues, but they had watched videos of me speaking and that had inspired them to take their own tough times in stride. I shared some of my own challenges with him, and before you know it, I had to remind him that he'd come to unlock my truck.

"Let me go get my tools," he said.

As I waited for him to return, the driver's door swung open. Implausibly, Romeo had unlocked the truck door! This is where my faith comes in: I believe that whole event happened for a reason. I didn't really need to watch the game that night —I needed to be out there, at that gas station, talking with that locksmith.

And the hits just keep on coming. On the Friday after Thanksgiving 2011, just a few days after the finale of *Dancing with the Stars*, my cell rang. I was at a lunch meeting with my literary agent.

"Hello?" I answered.

"Is this Mr. Martinez?" a woman asked.

Yes, it was, I told her.

"Please hold the line for a call from Defense Secretary Leon Panetta," she said.

I held the line.

A moment later Secretary Panetta came on. "Congratulations on your victory, Mr. Martinez," he said. He thanked me for speaking up on behalf of the troops and invited me to visit him the next time I was in Washington.

"Well, as a matter of fact, I'll be there next week," I said.

And that's how I found myself at the Pentagon, where I was welcomed like a conquering hero in an institution full of them. As I was escorted through the maze toward the secretary's office, men and women in uniform flowed out from every direction, slapping me on the back and congratulating me.

I was introduced to Deputy Defense Secretary Ashton B. Carter and Army General Martin E. Dempsey, chairman of the Joint Chiefs of Staff. General Raymond Odierno, the Army chief of staff, joked with me about *Dancing*. "I bet your fan base in the military gave you an extra edge to triumph over the Kardashians."

Never would I have imagined, back in 2002 as a nineteen-year-old private, that one day I'd be sharing a few yuks in the Pentagon with senior military leaders.

Finally it was time to see Secretary Panetta. I walked into his office, met his eyes, and did a little cha-cha step toward him. We spoke for a minute about the show and my victory, and I joked about showing him some dance steps. He politely declined. Then he thanked me again for speaking up for our troops overseas.

"I'm a soldier," I said, getting serious. "I'll always be a soldier, and I want to share the message from whatever platform I have. As the Department of Defense is hammering out ways to take care of our troops in different ways, I want to be able to find a way to express that to the general public."

Job well done, soldier, I told myself.

Then in April 2012 I had another chance to meet military royalty. I was invited by *Newsweek* magazine to be their guest at the White House Correspondents' Association dinner, probably the biggest night of the year in Washington. This year's event was as star-studded as usual, with comedian Jimmy Kimmel headlining and celebs like Kevin Spacey, Steven Spielberg, and Eva Longoria in attendance.

For me, the biggest thrill was being seated at the same table with General David Petraeus, current director of the CIA and, even more relevant to me, former commander of the 101st Airborne during the invasion of Iraq. He was friendly and personable, asking me what I was up to. When I told him I was working on this book, he mentioned his own newly published book, *All In*, and gave me a few pointers about navigating the editorial maze.

Taking my seat at the banquet table, I thought about calling Dan to tell him that I'd just shot the breeze with General Petraeus. Who could have ever imagined this? Nine years ago I was just an everyday soldier, and now I'd just had a personal conversation with one of the principals of recent history.

And now, like everyone else, it's time to think about what's next. I just turned twenty-nine and celebrated my first Father's Day. I still travel nonstop, which makes me appreciate my downtime at home all the more. I like nothing more than taking Romeo to the park or sitting around eating pizza and watching *SportsCenter*. I tell people that I will always stay grounded because if I ever get a big head, I'm brought right back to earth when I have to pick up that big dog's poop. Romeo adds so much to my life that I don't mind cleanup duty.

Another plus in my life is that I have a great relationship with Consuelo, who calls me "Renesito." A couple of years ago I traveled alone to El Salvador to visit her, and we became a lot closer. I love my sister and I want us to be a part of each other's lives. Someday I hope I can travel to Georgia to visit my mom and my sister, both living under the same roof. I'm working on it.

I also plan to work on a few things on my

bucket list. I want to learn to play piano again and try to surf. I want to go on a cruise and attend the Carnival in Rio. It's a dream to have my own jet so all that traveling I do is easier. I'd like to learn another language; I'm thinking Mandarin. And once things settle down, I'd finally like to go to college and get my degree. I enjoy motivating people, and I look forward to exploring future acting and entertainment opportunities.

So I'm different, but I'm still the same. I have lots of hopes and dreams. I continue to be very wary in my personal relationships. I have thousands of acquaintances but only a handful of really close friends. When I was a teenager, I thought people liked me because of my looks; after I was injured, I didn't know if people were being nice to me because they felt sorry for me. These days I sometimes wonder if people are trying to be close because I'm well known.

The one person I'll never have to worry about is my daughter. I want to watch her grow up; to be the father that I never had. I look forward to teaching her what I've learned, most importantly never to forget to have fun and laugh, because you never know what's around the corner.

ACKNOWLEDGMENTS

I want to first thank God for blessing me and those closest to me through all the tough times and guiding us through to positive outcomes. I want to thank him for my second chance at life, for giving me the opportunity to do the things I'm doing today, and for giving me the strength to do them. My faith has grown since my injury, and I believe, with faith, all is possible.

To the woman who never had the opportunity to be a child: I would like to thank my mother. She made incredible sacrifices to stay in the United States, even after learning her youngest daughter had passed away and her oldest daughter would have to remain in El Salvador. I am the way I am today because of my mother, and I admire her courage in facing so many obstacles to raise a boy on her own and take care of my sister and family in El Salvador. My mom has given me a lot, but the main thing is her smile. When people compliment me on my smile, I think of my mom's. I am the fighter I am because of you. This book is a tribute to my mother for being one badass woman—a four-foot, eleven-inch GIANT! I love you, Mom!

I want to acknowledge all of the soldiers who were with me in Iraq on April 5, 2003, especially Ernest Clayton, Justin Hart, Joshua Hopkins, Terrence O'Shea, and Chris Valdez. I hope they understand that this is my way of making the best of my second chance.

I would like to thank everyone at Brooke Army Medical Center in San Antonio. Their passion to care for me and every other burn patient is reflected in my life. I thank Dr. Dave Barillo, who worked on me tirelessly, saving my life. Big love to Mike Shiels and Bonnie Jackson, both nurses at BAMC who cared for me every day for months and, most important, became friends. I salute all of the staff at BAMC—doctors, nurses, therapists, civilians, Norma in public affairs, and so many more people—and to name everyone would mean I would need to write a separate book. Thank you all for your loving touches and for never allowing me to get stuck feeling sorry for myself, but instead encouraging me to keep placing one foot in front of the other.

Thanks to everyone in Dalton, who showed my mother and me an amazing amount of love since we first arrived. When my mother went to my side in the hospital, our community stepped up in a big way to sustain us—raising money to help my mom pay bills, sending messages of support, and being there for us every step of the way. Coach Ronnie McClurg and his wife, Judy; Ron and

Susan Ward; Mary Rose Threet and her husband, Gene: Thank you for being a big part of my life.

To my best friend, Dan Vargas, who lends his ears and shares his words in the moments when the rest of the world is asleep—he always answers his phone—and to the stories we've created together and the memories that will last forever: Cheers to you, my friend. Your friendship means the world to me.

To my former boss and great friend, Julie Carruthers: She believed in me, seeing something in me that ultimately allowed me to share it with the world.

Thanks to my girlfriend, Diana, who is someone I can always bounce ideas and thoughts off of. We started as friends and grew into so much more. You hold it down at home while I'm on the road. Thank you for understanding while I'm gallivanting around. The birth of our daughter, Lauryn Anabelle Martinez, or Belle, has added an incredible dimension to our lives.

To all of you who read this book, thank you for sharing this journey with me. I hope that every single one of you is able to take a message from the words in this book—something that will help you one day when you're facing adversity. Keep fighting! You will win if you keep at it.

—J. R. Martinez
Los Angeles

• • •

I would like to express my gratitude to J. R. Martinez, who trusted me to help tell his story, dug a little deeper every time he was asked, and could usually make me laugh!

I'm deeply indebted to Maria Felix Zavala, who spent seemingly limitless amounts of emotional energy to excavate her past so we could understand her journey. She also has the best giggle of anyone, anywhere.

This book would not have happened without the guidance of Robert Guinsler of Sterling Lord Literistic, Elizabeth Stein, and everyone at Hyperion. My appreciation to Major General Joseph Anderson for military and technical clarifications.

My thanks to everyone who graciously agreed to be interviewed, either for attribution or context; the professionals at BAMC; and Nancy Jeffrey at *People*, for giving me such great assignments, including the one at which I met J.R. Bouquets to Stefani McNair, Jana Dozier Sansbury, and Brenda Langston Sullivan for their critiques of the text.

An ocean of love to my family—siblings Bill Rockey and Alice Rockey, and my parents, Anna and retired Colonel William K. Rockey. My father, a thirty-one-year Marine Corps veteran, deserves special credit for vetting military references. My teenagers were understanding throughout the process and shouldered the burden of neglect and fast food without complaint. Thanks to my daughter, Natalie, whose compassion and intelligence will take her anywhere she wants to go, and my son, Garrett, who's a scholar, athlete, and the coolest guitar player I know. Love to Julie Norveel, who's been a ray of Norwegian sunshine this year, and always.

And love to the encyclopedic brains of the family, Dr. James M. Fleming, who is the voice of reason and who always has my back.

—Alexandra Rockey Fleming
Arlington, Virginia

Center Point Large Print

600 Brooks Road / PO Box 1
Thorndike ME 04986-0001 USA

(207) 568-3717

US & Canada:
1 800 929-9108
www.centerpointlargeprint.com